WHAT TEENS WANT YOU TO KNOW

What Teens Want You to Know

to Know

(but won't tell you)

Roy Petitfils

Franciscan
MEDIA
Cincinnati, Ohio

Scripture passages have been taken from *New Revised Standard Version Bible*, copyright ©1989 by the Division of Christian Education of the National Council of the Churches of Christ in the U.S.A., and used by permission. All rights reserved.

Cover design by Candle Light Studio
Cover image © istock I wakila
Book design by Mark Sullivan

LIBRARY OF CONGRESS CATALOGING-IN-PUBLICATION DATA
Petitfils, Roy.
What teens want you to know (but won›t tell you) / Roy Petitfils.
pages cm
ISBN 978-1-61636-222-5 (alk. paper)
1. Parent and teenager—Religious aspects—Christianity. 2. Adolescent psychology. I. Title.
BV4529.P437 2015
248.8'45—dc23
2014047105

ISBN 978-1-61636-222-5

Published by Franciscan Media
28 W. Liberty St.
Cincinnati, OH 45202
www.FranciscanMedia.org

Printed in the United States of America.
Printed on acid-free paper.
15 16 17 18 19   5 4 3 2 1

Contents

(*Foreword*)

I'm excited you're holding this book. I'm even more excited that Roy Petitfils wrote such a book.

I've been involved with teens for over thirty years, in varying roles of parent, teacher, coach, youth minister, and speaker. Sports teams, school clubs, classroom settings, youth conferences, and retreats have given me plenty of opportunities for chats with teens dealing with dating, friendships, self-image, family tensions, school pressures, media influences, college, the future, and more. I've heard slices of their lives, told with aloofness, excitement, drama, frustration, and anger. I've also listened to parents and teachers wonder if they are "doing it right" while helping teens through adolescence.

As insecure as some teenagers are about the issues they face, I've found there are also adults like me who wonder if we are really being of help and support to them. Many times, especially as a parent, I've thought: "I know something happened here, but I am not exactly sure what happened, why it happened, or if I responded well." I sense you might have some of the same thoughts—a desire for understanding and a desire to respond well to teens.

So thank you for picking up this book. Thanks for believing young people matter, for wanting to understand them better and respond to them well. That reassures me that I am not the only person who has questions or who wants to be a better companion to teens on their journey toward adulthood.

The poet T.S. Eliot said, "We had the experience but missed the meaning. / And approach to the meaning restores the experience in a different form."[1] That's what I believe you are holding in your hands now: a book that helps us reexamine our experiences, shed light on some meaning in those experiences, and reframe, through practical suggestions, ways to restore past experiences and equip us for future ones.

I'm excited that someone is helping us take a second look at these (often) emotional experiences with teens to help us see what might be going on under the surface (both for teens and for ourselves), and to give us some ideas for better ways to respond to these experiences. I'm excited that that someone is my friend, Roy Petitfils.

Roy and I have known each other for two decades. We've shared many of the same work and ministry experiences through those years, having attended the same college seminary (though a decade apart), been campus ministers at large, active, Catholic high schools, and now are both speakers on youth issues across the U.S. and Canada. We've shared stories, mistakes, and laughter about our ministries and our personal lives. We've picked one another's brains to see what we are learning about teens, about our faith, and about ourselves.

Roy is funny, filled with insight, compassion, and energy. As Mark Yaconelli said of his father, the great youth minister Mike Yaconelli, Roy is an elder with an adolescent heart. He brings a wealth of experience to this book as a teacher, campus minister, counselor, author, and speaker. He has done a great amount of self-exploration into his own adolescence, as well as spent countless hours listening and working with teens, parents, teachers, and other youth-serving agencies. He brings to his work a passion for helping people deal with the realities and emotions of everyday life.

Roy has many gifts, some of which you'll pick up within these pages. He is a wonderful raconteur, a person who tells anecdotes in a skillful and amusing way. There will be both humor and pain communicated richly as Roy shares stories, dialogue, and other reflections that can help us reexamine some of the awkward encounters we've had with teens, both past and present.

But Roy doesn't just tell nice stories. He helps us look past the complexity of teens' lives and realities (moodiness, non-communication, hormones, distancing, etc.) and works hard to name core needs of young people that are surfacing through their comments and behaviors. This is a gift in itself: to understand unspoken messages and needs that are often missed in our dealings with teens.

From there, Roy also gives practical hints to help us connect with young people in healthy ways as the terrain of adolescence is navigated. Roy blends reality with counseling and spiritual insights and common sense affirmations, challenges, and encouragements. I believe teens, parents, and even old friends like me can never get enough of that.

Thanks, Roy. Writing isn't as easy as it seems. I know what you went through to write this book. Well done.

May we all read this book with the intent of learning, understanding, and responding to the teens in our lives with generosity, faith, and love.

—*Mike Patin*
Pentecost, 2014

$$\left(Introduction\right)$$

It's reported that when Albert Einstein was teaching physics at Oxford University, one of his teaching assistants, in the middle of the spring final exam, barged into his office and said, "Professor, this is the identical final that you gave the students last semester."

As the story goes, Einstein looked over the test and said, "Yes, it is the same test." The teaching assistant knew, as anyone familiar with college life would, that if this was true, the students would have known and prepared for the questions used in the previous exam. And so the assistant repeated, "Professor, this test has the same questions as last year's exam!" Einstein replied, "Yes, but the answers have changed."

This concept is as true in working with teens as it is in the natural sciences—if not more so. Those of us who parent and work with teens are not asking any new questions. For the most part we're asking the same questions that have been asked since the dawn of time: "How do we raise happy, holy, healthy, successful kids?" "How do we protect our kids from the dangers of life?" Adults have been asking these questions for millennia, and we're no different. But, as Einstein understood, although we may be asking the same questions, the answers have changed.

When my mom, Connie Petitfils, asked the question, "How do I protect my son from life's dangers?" in the late 1970s, it merited a monumentally different answer than the one I hear when I ask that question today. In fact, the answer to that question ten years ago would have been drastically different than today. The same goes for five years ago, last year, last month—even yesterday.

The fact that teens are changing is not new; the pace at which their culture is changing, however, is new. This rate of change is unprecedented in the history of civilization. Despite momentous achievements and changes brought about by industrialization, technology, and automation, at no other point in history has there been such an explosive dynamic of change as what we're dealing with today.

That fact answers the question, "Why another book about teenagers?" It's not a bad question; part of me was concerned about publishing a book based on a subject that is changing drastically by the day—that is, how to relate to teenagers. In that sense, one might further ask, "What value could a resource such as this provide?"

Here are a few thoughts on those questions. In writing this book, I've drawn on twenty years of working with young people in a variety of settings: as a teacher, minister, administrator, and counselor in both parishes and schools, and today as a therapist in private practice, specializing in working with teens and families. Over the years I've learned general principles that were as true twenty years ago as they are today. I've learned tools that are effective in working with teenagers and that, when practiced, can adapt to shifting cultural trends. This is some of what I will share with you.

In this book you'll read the actual dialogue of counseling sessions with teens, parents, youth ministers, and educators. You'll hear the voices of real teens, along with their real concerns, fears, hopes, dreams, and needs. An important note here: in each case, names and other identifiable data have been modified to protect the confidentiality of those involved. In a few of these cases those modifications take the form of a composite that combines the story and traits of two or three individuals—not for dramatic effect, but to make one or more points more efficiently.

As you read through the book you'll notice that each chapter is filled with practical suggestions and ideas for you to use. Don't be overwhelmed by thinking you have to do them all. If everyone who reads this book each did one thing differently, stopped one unproductive behavior, or affirmed one thing he or she is already doing well, the state of relationships between teenagers and adults in our world would change dramatically.

You also may read some things where you think, "This won't work with my team. This will not be effective with the teens I work with." Trust that. You do not have to do everything suggested in the book. Instead, focus on what you feel will work with the teenagers in your life (although don't discount the value of trying something outside the box!).

On behalf of all the adults who spend their lives working with young people, with families, with parents—working to bridge the gap between the generations—thank you for picking up this book. Thank you for taking one step forward toward closing the ever-widening gap between teenagers and adults.

CHAPTER ONE (*Join Me: I Want a Relationship with You*)

+ Then little children were being brought to him in order that he might lay his hands on them and pray. The disciples spoke sternly to those who brought them; but Jesus said, "Let the little children come to me, and do not stop them; for it is to such as these that the kingdom of heaven belongs." And he laid his hands on them and went on his way. (Matthew 19:13–15)

+ We know that adults think we're weird, strange and...don't want to be around them. And I guess we are weird and perhaps strange, but we do want to be around adults. We do want to have deep, real conversations with adults. But I guess most of us, most of the time, see an adult as someone who is about to lecture us about stuff we already know.

—*A high school junior*

+ What kids need from adults is not just rides, pizza, chaperones, and discipline. They need the telling of stories, the close ongoing contact, so that they can learn to be accepted. If nobody is there to talk to, it is difficult to get the lessons of your own life so that you are adequately prepared to do the next thing. Without a link across generations, kids will only hear from their peers.... They want more regular contact with adults who care about and respect them.[2]

—*Patricia Hersch*

Jessica was a seventeen-year-old high school junior when she attended her class retreat. The second evening of the retreat was, according to the teens who had attended the retreat before, "heavy, deep, and real" and tended to be their favorite experience of the retreat. Students were beginning to lower their guard and trust one another and the adult leadership team.

Months before the retreat, I asked that their parents send me digital pictures of the teens when they were babies and as young children, doing something funny or slightly embarrassing. I then took the digital pictures and set them to music in a slideshow. During the retreat, as pictures of themselves, their parents, siblings, and friends flashed before their eyes, a previously rowdy group of adolescents grew still, legs crossed in perfect silence, eyes glued to the screen.

The point of this exercise was to jar teens out of their naturally self-conscious, preoccupied state to see themselves and others through a different lens. We wanted the students to look through the eyes of their parents or guardians and their God—those who gave them life, nurtured them, raised them, and helped them grow from the little children in those pictures into the young adults they were becoming.

Afterward the teens were separated into groups, and asked to process the experience by answering the question, "What was it like seeing yourself through your parent's eyes." Jessica, a member of my group, had tears streaming down her face. I looked at her and invited her to share what was on her mind. She said:

It was weird. I mean, it's like I never thought about it like that, you know? It's like I know (pointing to her head) my parents love me. They say it a lot, really. But I guess I don't think about them actually loving me (pointing to her heart). I know we always talk about how much we want to get away from our parents or want them to leave us alone, but down deep, that's not what we want. I do want my space and freedom. But I also want to spend time with my parents. It's just hard when all we talk about are things in my life that disappoint them—my grades, my friends, the way I dress, and my music. I wish they could see that I'm more than those things—not that those aren't important to me, but that I'm deeper than those things.

Jessica's feelings are not unique. I've heard this sentiment expressed by teens countless times. But I know that many adults—parents, teachers, clergy, and lay ministers, both professional and volunteer—would be shocked to hear this. This generally is not the impression given by the teens in their lives. In fact, it is the opposite.

Many adults feel as though they're doing teens a favor by giving them their space. In the words of one volunteer youth minister, "I can't tell you what a relief it is to hear this. I've been reading them [teens] wrong. This gives me hope that they do want me around and that I'm not just another authority figure they feel they have to rebel against."

In fact, and often unconsciously, teens can interpret that space as adults pulling away from them and feel abandoned. Other people don't get involved with youth ministry because they assume young people wouldn't come if they're around. One adult volunteer told me: "It has taken me years to volunteer to help with the youth ministry. I'd always assumed the kids wouldn't come if they knew adults were here."

Over time, I have learned that it isn't a case of whether or not we are present among teens, it's how we are present among them that makes all the difference. Most adults keep a safe distance from young people because they aren't privileged to see what I see and hear what I hear. Despite their words and behavior to the contrary, young people, more than anything else, desire a meaningful relationship with their parents and other significant adults.

Not only do younger generations want meaningful relationships with adults, but most adults I've known and worked with want with the same with young people. For a host of reasons these relationships do not exist in many homes, schools, and churches. Mutual fear and distrust is widening an already expansive crevasse between older and younger generations. Both sides are waiting for the other to take initiative in closing the gap. It's like two friends waiting for the other to take the first step to kiss and make up.

As adults it is our responsibility to take the initiative to close the gap. As Chap Clark says in *Hurt*, "Adolescents need adults. The problem is not that adults cannot reach adolescents. The problem is that adults have not invested the time, energy and commitment to reach adolescents."[3]

The responsibility to take the first step is ours. In general, adolescents do not have the strength and confidence to make such a move; their egos are still in the development stage. Compounding the difficulty for teens is the perceived power differential between youth and adults: the adults are on top and teens are on the bottom. It is unfair to expect them to reach up to us.

A parent once asked me, "Why must I reach out to them all the time? When is it their turn?" Behind this question lay love and frustration—love for a young person and frustration that the work of building a relationship with them feels one-sided, with adults doing all the work and teens not doing their part. This is understandable. Certainly, even relationships between teens and adults require work on both sides. But the initiative to close the generational gap and establish a healthy relationship is incumbent upon us.

We must reach out to them.

If we really want to share life and faith with teens, we must reach out to them. Chap Clark suggests, then, that we adults "must roll up our sleeves and go to adolescents, listen to them, and unconditionally care for them."[4]

Yet when most adults encounter a teen's resistance, they display one of three primary reactions: (1) sound the retreat and flee from the enemy, (2) charge in head first trying to change them without building a relational rapport, or (3) wave the white flag of surrender and try to be their buddy. None of these approaches works.

Over the last two decades our retreat from the adolescent world has not created a safer space between them and us. Instead, it most often creates a felt experience of abandonment. Teenagers don't want us to leave them alone, nor do they want us blasting down the door, storming into their lives with no regard for their privacy and autonomy. Finally, most teens have plenty of friends. They don't need another buddy.

REMAINING IN THE ROLE OF ADULT

One summer I taught religious education to a group of thirteen year olds. I charged in the first day with vigor and enthusiasm, determined that I, an overeducated, young, arrogant seminarian, would have these kids eating out of the palm of my hand. I was going to be hip, talk like them, and show them that I hadn't forgotten what it was like to be young.

"Wassup, yo?" I screamed as I swung open the door, barged into the room, and did what I thought to be a cool move with my hands. This caused two girls to dive under their desks screaming and two boys to nearly choke to death laughing at me, while the rest of the class sat there stunned, shocked, and embarrassed—for me. My attempt to "be hip," as they would later describe the scene, resembled (I quote) a "wounded sea lion trying to break dance." They were not impressed at all by my attempts to be cool. I came off as inauthentic (which was true) and as trying too hard to get them to like me (which was also true).

Teens are people savvy. Too often we don't give them enough credit. They sense insecurity, fear, and low self-esteem. They are astute practitioners who recognize it, name it, and call it out—especially in adults.

At the time I thought I needed teens to like me in order to share Christ with them. But earning the respect of teens is far more valuable than having them like you. You don't have to try to get them to respect you. It's something you earn by remaining true to yourself and showing them the same respect you would like from them.

I once invited an adult volunteer, Alex, to give a talk at a retreat. I knew Alex was a faith-filled man with incredible depth, and I wanted the teens to experience what he had to offer. But he was very soft spoken and in no way a dynamic speaker. I was concerned that he wouldn't be able to grab and hold the teens' attention for forty minutes after lunch on the first day. I was also concerned that his message might be too deep for my teens. Nevertheless, I made arrangements with Alex to speak at the retreat.

After slowly making his way to the podium and deliberately arranging his notes, he raised his head, looked the teens in their eyes, then gave a nervous, sheepish grin. A few teens started chuckling, and my heart began pounding. I thought, "This is going south so fast, and I can't stop it." Alex began by telling a corny Cajun joke, and within two minutes the whole room was laughing—with him. He then told his faith story in a natural, humble way.

When Alex had finished talking, the teens gave him a standing ovation. Afterward, many remarked that it was the highlight of the retreat. The content of Alex's talk wasn't nearly as remarkable as how he gave it. Alex didn't try to get the teens to like or respect him. He captured their attention by being appropriately transparent, genuine, and self-confident. If I had told the same joke, no one would have laughed because I don't tell jokes well. If I'd given a talk in the same way he had, it would have fallen flat because I'm a naturally dynamic, expressive speaker.

Alex's talk worked because he did three things really well:

1. *There was appropriate transparency.* There's a balance to be achieved here. On one end it is essential that teens know enough about us to experience us as a real person. On the other end, total transparency by an adult to a group of young people is rarely appropriate. Even today, with almost twenty years of experience working with young people, I often consult others to check the appropriateness of any personal information I intend to share with young people. You should do the same.

2. *He was authentic.* Be yourself. Although we tell teens this all the time, it amazes me how few adults really believe it. God has uniquely created each one of us. If we believe this, then we don't need to try to be like anyone else other than who we are. This is attractive to young people; being someone or something other than who or what we are is not.

3. *He was respectful of the teens.* Too often we underestimate the range of emotional and spiritual experiences teens have. Bob McCarty, director of the National Federation of Catholic Youth Ministry and one of my mentors, has often noted that teens are experience rich and language poor. When in doubt about the level of depth in your sharing, go deeper rather than shallower. Better to risk missing the mark by going too deep than patronizing teenagers by being too shallow.

Teens want and need adults to be grounded in being adults. When your goal is to be liked by young people your risk losing sight of the bigger goal, which is to journey with them into Christian maturity. Secondly, you'll lose the respect of teens, which is worth a lot more than being liked. The key to effectively reaching them and deepening our relationships with them is not by trying to be their friend, but by being friendly, authentic, and respectful to them while maintaining healthy boundaries as an adult.

Deep down, we all want to be liked; there's nothing wrong with that. In fact, it is perfectly normal. I've never met a person who will not eventually admit they want other people to like them.

When people like us we tend to feel more secure and safe, both with ourselves and in the relationship. We must be mindful, however, that our natural desire to be liked by others may not be beneficial to our relationships with teenagers—whether we are a parent, minister, or teacher. The energy you invest in being a parent, mentor, and leader will pay off when your teens are adults, and you can begin to establish a mature, adult friendship.

POINTS TO REMEMBER
- Despite the generational distance between teens and adults—as well as what their behavior might indicate—teenagers do want meaningful relationships with adults.
- Be appropriately transparent, authentic, and respectful when working with teenagers.
- Whether you're parenting, teaching, or ministering to teens, it is normal to want to be liked by them, but it is more important to remain grounded in your role as an adult.

QUESTIONS FOR REFLECTION
1. What is one positive attribute you see in teens today? Is there an attribute that you don't understand or don't like? Why?
2. What makes it difficult for you to relate to young people today?
3. If you could share one thing with teens today that you know would reach them, what would it be? Why?

4. Knowing that teens want a meaningful relationship with adults, what's one thing you can do, change, or stop doing to make your relationship with a teen in your life more meaningful?

5. What is the best way to earn someone's respect? Reflect on a time in your life when you sought someone's respect and did or did not get it.

PRAYER

Lord Jesus, you humbled yourself and took on our human nature. With you as our model, may we humble ourselves and reach out to our young people. Give us courage as we face the sharp edges of their personalities and multiple defenses so that we might bridge the gap between us, and in so doing share the Good News with them. Amen.

CHAPTER TWO (*Hear Me and I Will Listen*)

+ If I speak in the tongues of mortals and of angels, but do not have love, I am a noisy gong or a clanging cymbal. And if I have prophetic powers, and understand all mysteries and all knowledge, and if I have all faith, so as to remove mountains, but do not have love, I am nothing. If I give away all my possessions, and if I hand over my body so that I may boast, but do not have love, I gain nothing. (1 Corinthians 13:1–3)

+ You may not think I paid attention in your class, but I did. And I did—we did—because we knew you cared about us more than you cared about our religion book or what was in it. We felt safe to be who we were and think what we thought. And because of that we really listened to what you had to say.

     —*A teen reflecting on her ninth-grade religious ed class*

+ When we enter into the lives of young people, truly listen to them, accompany them through their struggles, we begin to understand their spiritual hungers. Whether it's the hunger for love, belonging, purpose, completion, forgiveness, or to make a difference, Jesus is the match to their hunger. [5]

     —*Frank Mercadante*

I first got to know Jeanne when she was sixteen years old. She was a sophomore in high school and battling bulimia, an eating disorder. Before she came to see me, she had seen two other counselors who were specialists in treating eating disorders.

When Jeanne came into my office that first day, her look said it all: "I've been around, man. There's nothing you're gonna say or do that's gonna get me to open up and let you in. Don't waste your time." To her, I was just another talking head at the end of a line of talking heads who were happy to take her parents' money and try to get her to put on weight, just another person who was getting paid to fix her. She had little use for me.

With a crucifix on my wall and the fact that I was a proclaimed Catholic counselor, Jeanne had me pegged. In her mind, not only was I going to try to shove food down her throat, but Jesus too! And after ten years of religious ed classes, she'd just about had enough of people trying to force Jesus and the Church on her. She looked at me as if to say, "Go ahead. I dare you to try and figure me out, big boy."

But none of that was my intention in seeing Jeanne. I really liked her from the start, and while I didn't want her to remain in the throes of bulimia, first I wanted to get to know her better. I didn't want to fix her, as I was pretty sure she, like me, wasn't defective or damaged goods. I was more concerned about who or what had hurt her or let her down. The rest was just details.

I started our session by asking Jeanne what she was interested in—what her hobbies were, what she liked to do for fun, who her friends were. It was all basic stuff to build rapport, because I knew that if it seemed like I was trying to help Jeanne or fix her, she would retreat further into her shell and make it even more difficult for me—or anyone else—to help her.

At the end of our first session, I offered Jeanne a deal: if I promised not to counsel her (as she would define it), she would continue to show up once a week until her parents or me decided to end the therapy. I told her parents privately that if her situation became more urgent than simply needing a weekly session with me, I'd refer her for residential treatment. (She was also seeing a doctor and a nutritionist.)

During Jeanne's sessions over the next few weeks, we talked about music, people, life, food, drugs, religion, and life in general. Each of these conversations was a little trust test. Jeanne would talk about a risqué subject, or make an inflammatory remark with a liberal dose of vulgarity, just to see my response. After a few weeks of this, I knew that I'd passed the test when she unlocked the door with this question "So I guess you're gonna tell me to stop purging, huh?" I responded, "Nope. I have no intention of doing that."

"Yeah, right," she said, looking away.

I told her, "I'm guessing you've had plenty of people, including your parents and other counselors, telling you to stop purging, accompanied by a litany of reasons why you should." She looked at me quizzically, as I continued, "So that's covered: Make client aware that adults don't want her to purge. Check."

After pausing for a few moments I asked, "What do you want—for you?"

"I dunno. I never thought about that." She shrugged and looked away, then continued in a softer voice, "I guess, what everyone wants, to be happy."

"What does happiness mean for you?"

"I dunno."

I handed Jeanne my laptop, which was open on a blank page, and asked if she could type the answer. She then typed an entire page—single-spaced—about happiness. In those sentences and paragraphs were the seeds for every conversation we would have over the next two years.

I asked Jeanne's permission to print out the document, and whether or not she would be interested in talking about what she wrote. She said, "Yeah, sure." I printed two copies, and handed one to her, noting, "You wrote down a lot of important things here. And while we'll get to all of them eventually, we'll only have time to talk about one or two today. Where would you like to start?"

It was no surprise to me when Jeanne wanted to talk about her boyfriend, because, as she said, "He makes me happy."

I asked, "What about him makes you happy?"

"He's there for me," she said, and with depth and conviction looked me right in the eye.

"It means a lot to you when someone's 'there for you'?"

"Mmm hmm," she mumbled.

"What does it mean to 'be there' for someone?"

"It means that they love you no matter what. That when things go bad you can count on them."

"It sounds like your boyfriend has been there for you during a bad time in your life," I said.

"Uh huh. And he still is."

"Is this still a bad time in your life?"

"Yeah."

"So you're going through a hard time in your life right now and your boyfriend is there for you."

"Yeah."

At this point Jeanne began to visibly soften in her tone of voice, facial expressions, and body language, unfolding her arms. She was beginning to lower her guard and trust me because she felt that her feelings were validated.

During our discussions I made it a point to mirror, or reflect back to Jeanne what I was getting from her. "I can tell you really don't want to be here. If I were you I might feel the same way." "So you think Justin Timberlake is hot? What do you like about him?" "It's important for you to look good, isn't it?" I did this "dance" with her for three weeks. She would say something, pick a topic for discussion, and I would reflect it back to her after a bit of mutual banter. I might have said something like this as well, "I don't get Justin Timberlake. Help me understand what's so compelling about him. Why are people so crazy about him?"

In various ways, I continued to talk about what was important to her and why it was important. If there had been any attempt on my part to shift the conversation to Jeanne's eating disorder she would have seen right through it, because teens have an incredibly accurate detector for insincerity, inauthenticity, and adult agendas. Further, she would have retreated back because the eating disorder would have been seen as my agenda, not something that was important to her. I would have gone back on my word and be seen as trying to counsel her.

Because the focus of our discussions remained on what was important to her, and I empathized and reflected back to her both verbally and nonverbally, she eventually came to feel that she was being heard. Everyone desires to feel heard. It is an experience of intimacy when we feel that another "gets us," and it's amazing what lengths people will go to in order to feel heard.

At every point in our lives, but most especially during the turbulent period of adolescence, we desire to be known and understood in some way. This is true for every teen, although teenagers who are hurt and wounded experience this desire more intensely. Because of this, they will guard both themselves and their hearts very carefully from anyone they fear or suspect will hurt them.

BUILD RAPPORT

One important element in building a relationship with Jeanne and convincing her that I was willing to listen to her was that I paid attention to her from the first moment she entered my office, noting her facial expressions, body language, tone of voice, rolling eyes, and manner of dressing. All of this communicated clearly to me that she was disgusted with her parents for bringing her to another counselor. My office was the last place she wanted to be.

We must build rapport and earn the right to be heard with adolescents today, who largely are skeptical and distrustful of adults. That's what happened in Jeanne's case. Her two previous counselors either skipped over or tried to rush through building a rapport with her. They rolled up their sleeves and got right down to the work of trying to fix her. That mistake cost them the opportunity to journey with an amazing young woman along the path to healing.

When you're tired, busy, overwhelmed, afraid, nervous, in a hurry, or feel pressured to make something happen, the first thing that usually goes out the window is your willingness to empathize and express compassion. Feeling like you need to "get it over with," "make something happen," or, "move past this," are normal. It takes a lot of energy to empathize, to intentionally move out of the space from which you view the world into a teenager's space so you can see life through their eyes.

It seems much more efficient to bark, "Go clean your room!" or preach from a list of "thou shall nots," hoping that this will deliver the desired result. Yet the reality is that these methods are seldom effective with teens today. Either we accept that reality and work toward being more empathetic, hearing what our teens need to say, or we remain in denial and continue to spout platitudes.

Unless you spend a lot of time with adolescents, observing them, interacting with them, and studying them, it's best not to assume you know what's important to them. That's likely what occurred with Jeanne. One or both counselors mistakenly assumed that treating her eating disorder was important to Jeanne. It was not. What was important to Jeanne was that someone "got" her and was there for her, like her boyfriend.

Treating the eating disorder was important to Jeanne's parents, who were paying the bill for her therapy, and it was important to the therapist for that reason—as well as for Jeanne's overall health and well-being. Yet when it came to having the opportunity to influence Jeanne in a positive way, what mattered is what she perceived as important.

Here are a few principles that guided me and enabled me to really listen and hear what Jeanne needed to say:

Use an indirect approach. I decided not to directly address Jeanne's bulimia at least initially because I knew she didn't want to talk about it. Sometimes tackling issues head on doesn't work because the person is not ready to admit or work through a particular problem or issue.

Focus and refocus on what the teen really wants. I asked Jeanne what she wanted, and listened to what she had to say, implicitly giving her permission to express her feelings. Too often, without realizing it, we lose sight of this important principle. People, teens especially, will address what's important to them. It's easy to lose sight of this and spend a lot of time trying to get a teen to work on something that may be important to you and their parents, but not to them.

Ask and ask again "So, help me understand why this is so important to you." By doing this we give the teen an opportunity to realize, often for the first time, why certain experiences, opinions, and stances are important to them.

Understand that as an adult, you are in a powerful position, and take the initiative to give the teen a sense of control and autonomy within the relationship. I allowed Jeanne to feel in control of our interaction by mirroring back to her what she was saying, and let her correct me if I seemed to misunderstand.

From time to time, I would ask Jeanne if she felt she was being heard. Jeanne usually responded that she did feel she was being heard, and in time came to believe that I understood her. That was valuable to her and was clearly a new experience. This did not happen immediately; I didn't get to decide when she would lower her guard. Only she could decide that. As I would later find out, the sense that she had some control over the counseling session was one of the few things in Jeanne's life she could take ownership of. If I took that away, I would never have had an opportunity to address the deeper issues fueling her eating disorder.

You probably are not a professional counselor, and I don't want to turn you into one (although in some ways anyone who interacts with teens takes on that role at times). But the general principles that I used in my interactions with Jeanne can help you be a more effective parent, teacher, or minister.

POINTS TO REMEMBER
- Adults must earn the right to be heard by teens. Teens will listen to us when we invest time listening to them.
- The only way you'll know if you're hearing what teens need to say is by asking, "Do you feel heard?" Ask this question whenever you're not sure if you're hearing everything they have to say, and then follow up with, "What am I (or your parents, friends, boyfriend, girlfriend, God) not hearing?"
- Giving teens a sense of power in relationships allows them to feel less threatened and safer with you.

QUESTIONS FOR REFLECTION

1. Who is someone who really listens to you? How do you feel when someone finally "gets" you?

2. What is one thing you can begin doing today to be a better listener?

3. Who is someone you know that is really good at building rapport with teens? What do they do differently? Ask this person, "I see you as someone who is gifted at connecting with teens. If there were one or two things you would offer someone wanting to connect better with teens, what would it be?"

PRAYER

Lord, remind us often that you love our young people more than we can. Teach us how to love the young people in our lives, especially when they seem to reject our imperfect attempts to love them. We pray to you through the intercession of your beloved St. Francis of Assisi, who sought first to understand before being understood. Amen.

CHAPTER THREE (*See Me through My Masks*)

+ Jesus, looking at him, loved him and said, "You lack one thing; go, sell what you own, and give the money to the poor, and you will have treasure in heaven; then come, follow me." (Mark 10:21)

+ Sure people see me, but they don't really "see" me. They see parts of me, the athlete, the guy who likes to party, the stud who gets the girls. They don't see the depressed kid who hates his life, who feels pressured into living up to a reputation he created, and the part of me that's scared to death of someone finding out about these "other" parts of me.

—High school junior boy

+ Youth need our appreciative gaze; mostly they simply need our gaze. One of the deepest hungers inside young people is the hunger for adult connection, the desire to be recognized, seen, by a significant adult.... They desperately need, and badly want, the blessing that comes from our gaze and presence. They need for us to see them. In the end, more than they want our words, they want our gaze.[6]

—Ronald Rolheiser, O.M.I.

Like many teens I've worked with, I didn't grow up in the most functional of families. I was born to a single mother who worked three or four jobs at any given point to make ends meet. Most nights she worked late. From the age of thirteen onward I spent many weeknights home alone in an empty house feeling lonely, sad, and angry. Of course I couldn't articulate that at thirteen, but I was hurting, and I wanted to make the hurt go away. I turned to food.

Every day I would come home and try to eat things that made me feel better. And week by week, month by month, I was needing more and more food to make me feel better. By the age of fifteen I could no longer be weighed on my doctor's scale, which maxed out at 350 pounds, and I was forced to be weighed on a scale at our local butcher shop. As I stood on the steel platform and watched the long red needle spin and land at 420, I murmured "That can't be right." My mom, with tears in her eyes, assured me we would do something about my weight. We didn't.

Being a poor kid on scholarship at a private school was hard enough on its own. Being morbidly obese didn't help. It felt as though I was picked on constantly. And the more I got teased the more I ate when I got home. By the time I was a senior in high school I couldn't fit in the desks in several of my classes and those that I did squeeze into left welts and bruises on my stomach and side. Wearing a 6X shirt and size 64-inch waist, now weighing 480 pounds, I was embarrassed to leave the house and almost never wanted to go to school.

Midway into my senior year a teacher pulled me aside and informed me that I was becoming obnoxious, which wasn't like me, and he wondered what was going on. I had no idea what he was talking about. I told my mom, and she suggested that I be nicer to people. I didn't realize I wasn't being nice.

Today I attribute that obnoxious attitude largely to my desire to be seen. At some point during high school I stopped getting picked on. I went from being bullied to being ignored. As strange as it may sound, being harassed was preferable to feeling ignored. I was the biggest human being in my town, yet most days I felt like no one could see me. Unconsciously, I left behind Mr. Nice and ushered in Mr. Jerk. Mr. Nice was invisible. Mr. Jerk got me attention—negative attention, to be sure, but at least that was something.

Rejection, contrary to what many suggest, is not our greatest fear: being invisible is. I've experienced in my own life and in the lives of teens I know that rejection is preferable to not feeling that you are seen. We need attention, especially during our formative years, and we'll stop at nothing to get it—even if it means attracting negative attention.

People will get as big as it takes (through food or steroids), as thin as it takes, have as many piercings and tattoos as it takes, wear whatever hairstyle and clothing it takes, and act in whatever way necessary to receive attention. For teens, attention is like oxygen to the soul. And in the most unfortunate situations they'll take lives, including their own, so as to not feel invisible. It's no wonder that as of this writing, suicide is the third leading cause of death for teenagers today.[7] If I can't be seen, then why should I be here at all?

SEEING THE WHOLE

Sometimes it's not that teens feel totally invisible, like I did, but that they feel a certain part of them is not being seen. Such was the case with Stephen, a high school junior who, on paper, had every reason to be happy. He was a great athlete, and he had a wonderful personality and lots of friends. His parents were genuinely kind, warm, and delightful people—to which he would attest. On the surface, it didn't make sense at all that this young man was depressed, having suicidal thoughts, always irritable, and now verbally lashing out toward his parents.

When we first met for counseling, he was smiling and very friendly, which is rare in teens at the first session. We seemed to hit if off right away, and he didn't hesitate to tell me that he hadn't been feeling like himself lately. In fact, he wasn't sure what that even felt like anymore. He was aware that he was losing his temper with his parents, and starting to do the same with peers and teachers. But he couldn't figure out why.

Just as I was about to bring the session to a close, with three minutes left, he said, "Oh, and I'm adopted."

I said nothing and just looked into his eyes. Knowing how important it is, for guys especially, not to feel overexposed too soon, I broke eye contact and asked "What's it like for you—being adopted?"

"It sucks!" he said harshly as if I, the counselor, was an expert who should know that being adopted sucks.

"So," I said, "For you being adopted is a really tough thing."

"Yeah. It is," he said and then stood up, smiled, shook my hand, and said while walking out the door, "See you next week, man."

I began our second session by asking, "What was it like for you last time? When you left my office, what were you feeling? Thinking?"

"Well," he paused, "I dunno. I mean, I guess it was good."

"But what were you feeling when you left?" I said.

"Oh...relieved, I think," he said, looking away.

"What happened last time that made you feel relieved?" I asked.

Stephen paused and then said, "I think it was the way you looked at me when I told you I was adopted. I don't know what I was expecting, but I'm always scared to tell people I'm adopted. Either they look at me like an orphan or they try to convince me that I'm better off than I could be, and that I should be grateful to have such wonderful parents and a wonderful life, considering my alternative.

But you didn't do that. You just looked at me for a while and asked what being adopted was like for me. That was cool."

In the following weeks and months Stephen shared with me how he was picked on as a kid for being adopted. He would cringe as he recounted stories of kids in middle school calling him a "redhead orphan." Stephen allowed me to walk with him toward healing those painful wounds because in our first visit he experienced me seeing a part of him that others did not, but a part he wished they would. Even though he was aware of his many blessings and grateful for much of his current life, there was a part of him that felt neglected, unworthy, and unwanted.

In Sue Monk Kidd's novel *The Secret Life of Bees*, August Boatwright, a black woman who farms bees for honey, takes in Lily, a girl who has run away from her abusive, single father. Lily soon discovers that ironically, this was the same place her mother ended up when she left Lily's dad years ago.

Lily struggles to understand why her mom would leave her, and August suggests that when people are hurting they need to leave the situation they believe is hurting them. Lily responds "Was it the wounded places down inside people that sought each other out, that bred a kind of love between them?" To which August responds, "But it's something everybody wants—for someone to see the hurt done to them and set it down like it matters."[8]

Teens need us to see their pain, even if there has been no perceived harm done to them. It may be that they experienced a particular situation as painful or that there was a relationship or time in their life that caused them hurt. During these times, what they need most is not someone's logical explanation of how they see the situation, but validation. Rather than making the person feel like a victim, this validation legitimizes their experience and shines the light of hope into their darkness. It offers meaning to what would otherwise feel like a random, possibly sadistic experience.

In Mark's account of Jesus's interaction with a wealthy young man, (Mark 10:17–22), it reads "Jesus, looking at him, loved him." Jesus made it a point to see that young man, and in so doing loved him in such a powerful way. The French word used in this passage is *regarder*, a verb that means "to watch." In my personal Bible, I've written the word "regarding" over the words "looking at" in this passage. It says a bit more. It speaks of a respectful, attentive look. In fact, when we don't feel respected and attended to we use the word "disregarded."

I often wonder what the young man felt as Jesus gazed at him. When I was nineteen, I believe I experienced that gaze. By my second year of college, I was weighing in at over five hundred pounds. One day, bribing me with hot donuts, some friends persuaded me to visit the Catholic student center on campus. While sitting on a sofa eating donuts right out of the box, a Catholic priest walked up to me and introduced himself. At that point, I hadn't darkened the door of a church in five years, and I dreaded conversing with a man of the cloth. I didn't want to give him my spiritual resume or have to lie to him if he asked me about going to Mass when I had no intention of doing so.

The priest looked deep into my eyes and smiled in a way that no one had ever smiled at me before. Instead of asking me to attend Mass, he invited me to lunch. After that lunch, he invited me to another, and another. At least once a week throughout the Fall and Spring semesters, he invited me to spend time with him, usually at a local pizzeria sharing its signature meat pizza called the "T-Rex." I remember feeling, "This guy doesn't seem to notice that I'm obese and poor."

Today I realize that he did notice, but that didn't throw him off, because he saw something deeper in me. When I was a 500-pound 19-year-old he saw the 220-pound healthy, 41-year-old husband and father who is writing this book. He saw the entrepreneur, the minister I could and would grow to become. He saw me. The way he saw me affected the way he treated me, and the way he treated me drastically affected the course of my life. I can say without question that I am who I am and where I am today as a direct result of being truly seen by him and by a few others at the Catholic student center. How we see others matters.

The young man in the Gospel ultimately walks away sad because he had many possessions. I've read and heard interpretations of this Gospel story that assume the young man spent the rest of his life off track, that he left Jesus with no intention of ever doing what Jesus asked—"sell what you own, and give the money to the poor, and you will have treasure in heaven; then come, follow me" (Mark 10:21).

But since the details of what happens to the young man after he leaves, disappointed in Jesus's answer, are not known, I'd like to think that at some point in his life, the man was touched by the way Jesus saw him and did indeed turn his life over to Christ.

Here are a few practical tips for "seeing" teens:

Be aware of your assumptions. As much as possible begin every interaction with an open mind. This is not easy, but it's difficult to see the reality of the young person in front of us when our vision is being blurred by our preconceptions and assumptions. Adolescence is a time of rapid change on every level. When I was teaching in the classroom, every day I had a note on my desk that read, "These are not the same kids that were here yesterday; get to know these kids."

Make and keep eye contact. I know, it sounds too simple actually to be effective, but I've found this to be a very useful tool in counseling, mentoring, and parenting. The reason it's so effective, especially today, is that many teens spend their days looking into their cell phones, tablets, computers, and the like. The amount of real eye contact they experience is minimal. So when you do engage with teenagers in this way, it has an impact on the person, even if only unconsciously.

Smile. The majority of teens today are wary of adults. They don't necessarily assume that we're mean or out to get them, they just don't tend to trust us. A genuine smile tells them we're not the enemy. It also tells them they are someone worth smiling at.

Ask open-ended questions and listen. Even if their answers are brief or they act a little weird about this, it is usually because they are nervous. But teenagers like the attention, and appreciate your effort to let them know you care about what they think. When we make a habit of asking them questions and then patiently listening to them while they answer, teens feel seen. They experience this as us focusing on them in a positive way, and it contributes to their positive self-esteem. It's another opportunity to build trust and a pathway for open communication.

Times have changed, and teens in some very important respects are different than I was as a teen—as you were as a teen. But that desire to be seen remains constant. The experience of being seen by another is a powerful form of intimacy. Deep inside each of us, at every point in our lives, but most especially during the turbulent period of adolescence, we need to be seen. Teens need to see themselves through the eyes of significant others. When this happens we feel known, understood in some way. This is especially important for teens who have been wounded. What may seem like a distrust of others is usually matched by an equal desire to be really seen.

POINTS TO REMEMBER
- How we look at people, how we see them, matters greatly. This is especially true for teenagers.

- We do not come to love ourselves in a vacuum. We come to love ourselves by seeing ourselves as loveable through the eyes of others.
- Adults play a crucial role in establishing a foundation for healthy self-love and respect in teens. This starts with the way we perceive them.
- It is common for teens, even in an age of unprecedented accessibility, to feel as though some or many people close to them, do not really see them.
- Ask teens, "If there was something about you, in you, that you wish people saw but don't, what would that be? Who would you want to see that?

QUESTIONS FOR REFLECTION

1. Who was someone, during your teen years, who really saw you? What difference did it make in your life?
2. Who is a teen in your life now that you sense needs to be seen? How might you approach them in order to see them better?
3. What gets in the way of you seeing teens in your life?

PRAYER

Lord help us to really see deep into the hearts of teens, in the same way you search and probe our own hearts. Give us the grace to want to see you and your Spirit as you dwell within each of the teens in my life. Amen.

CHAPTER FOUR

(*Reach Me through My Resistance*)

+ I therefore, the prisoner in the Lord, beg you to lead a life worthy of the calling to which you have been called, with all humility and gentleness, with patience, bearing with one another in love, making every effort to maintain the unity of the Spirit in the bond of peace. (Ephesians 4:1–3)

+ I know we are tough to reach sometimes. But deep down, we want you guys to push through. I know, I know we make it hard and even say we don't want it [a relationship with adults]. But most of us don't mean it. I guess—we just want to see how much you care. How hard are you willing to work? How long are y'all willing to stick with us?

  —*High school senior girl*

+ Bee yard etiquette: ...the world is really one big bee yard, and the same rules work fine in both places: Don't be afraid, as no life-loving bee wants to sting you. Still, don't be an idiot; wear long sleeves and long pants. Don't swat. Don't even think about swatting. If you feel angry, whistle. Anger agitates, while whistling melts a bee's temper. Act like you know what you're doing, even if you don't. Above all, send the bees love. Every little thing wants to be loved.[9]

  —*Sue Monk Kidd*

When I met Alex, a sixteen-year-old high school sophomore, and his mother in the waiting room of my counseling office, everything about him said, "I'm never going to talk to you. I hate you. I hate this place. I hate my mother for bringing me here." In a previous conversation with Alex's mom, she warned me he would be difficult, as he was convinced that he didn't need to see a therapist. He had told her if she dared bring him to one she would be wasting her money, because he had no intention of talking.

Once in my office, Alex assumed his slumped position and began fiddling with his phone, communicating that he planned on ignoring me. This irritated me. At this point in my career I'd worked with some pretty resistant teens; this teen was not only resistant, he was being rude. As I sat with Alex, I noticed my frustration at his disrespect. I thought, "It's one thing to not talk, it's another to nonverbally tell me to 'go fly a kite.'" He was doing both. I hate admitting this, but I started with, "Look kid, if you don't want to talk, I ain't gonna make you. We can just sit here and waste your mom's money."

And that's exactly what we did. After twenty minutes of silence I tried a pep talk: "You know, counseling could really be helpful to you," to which he sighed and then silently chuckled. I tried to be hip and cool, asking what he was playing on his phone—no response.

After thirty minutes of flailing around, I said, "Alex, I give up man. I have to give it to you, you're one of the toughest teens I've ever worked with. I pride myself on being someone teens want to talk to, but it's clear to me you're not like most teens, even most teens who are forced to see a counselor. I respect your decision to not talk—and the more I think about it, and try to put myself in your situation, I might have done the same thing if my mom had brought me to see a therapist against my will. But before we go, help me understand something: Why is it so important to you to not talk?"

"Because that would make her [his mother] right," he said.

"Make her right about what?" I asked.

"About needing to see a therapist. If I talk to you, she'll win, and she always wins."

"So if you talk to me, she wins and you lose?"

"Exactly," he muttered.

"So, what if…" (I took a long pause, waiting for him to grow impatient and acknowledge he wanted to hear what I was going to say).

"What if what?"

"What if—and I'm not saying there is—but what if there was a way for you to walk out of here with a win and also talk with me?"

"I dunno," he said.

I waited for him to say more. Usually when teens say, "I dunno," it means they are processing what you asked them and need more time to think about their response.

"I don't see how that's gonna happen."

"Me either, right away but what if it were possible?"

"I guess that would be alright."

"So what do you need in order to walk out of here with a win today?"

"I need my mom to know I didn't talk to you."

"Deal. I'll tell your mom we didn't have a meaningful conversation and that you were the toughest teen I've ever worked with. And I'll reschedule with her for next week, stating I'd like to give it one more try, and we can take it from there. How does that sound?"

"I guess that's OK."

We shook hands and Alex walked into the waiting room. I did as I told him I would, which was true, and allowed Alex to save face and have a sense of control within his relationship with his mom.

The following week we began where we left off. I was able to get Alex to agree to talk with me under the condition that, for the next few weeks, his mother must agree to not ask him about therapy. I told him eventually I'd need to talk with her, but I could do that by myself and not break his confidence. He was OK with this arrangement.

In future sessions, Alex eventually opened up as I earned his trust and created a way for him to save face with his mom. He would eventually set and attain a goal of having a better relationship with his mom, characterized by open communication. None of this would have happened if I had taken Alex's resistance personally. His resistance was not about me; it was about his mom. I also had to learn that the resistance wasn't all in Alex. I was contributing toward that stalemate as well. My expectations of him to willingly talk and be like all the other tough teens I've worked with was getting in the way of me understanding Alex.

In this chapter we'll explore the nature of resistance, how we as adults contribute to it and tips and strategies on how to roll with the resistance instead of fighting it, which will give us unique opportunities to influence teenagers.

Simply put, resistance is anything that interferes with having a meaningful relationship with the teens in your life. Resistance appears in the form of a kid who rolls his eyes when you ask him to do something or in the incredulous look that surfaces on a teen's face when you're talking about something they disagree with or in the sarcastic, skeptical, or critical comeback they make when you tell them to do something they don't want to do. It would be a mistake, however, to assume that resistance is only present in adolescents.

To our detriment, we have assumed that the resistance is in the adolescent. To an extent, that is true. But it is even truer that resistance is what occurs between you and an adolescent. If you want to effectively form influential relationships with teens, you must accept responsibility for the attitudes, beliefs, and the behaviors that fuel this relationship. This is not about blame or finding fault. This is about taking the initiative. If we're taking the initiative in forming a healthy relationship with a teen, which we should, then we must take that same initiative in acknowledging our role in creating resistance when it occurs. Resistance lowers our ability to influence teens.

The most effective way to affect an undesirable behavior in a teen is to practice radical acceptance of that behavior before trying to influence or change that behavior.

Recognizing Resistance
Whenever we find ourselves trying to get teens to do something, believe something, choose something, or value something, and they choose not to do it, there is resistance. In the story about Jeanne told in chapter two, she had clearly communicated to me, mostly without words, that she did not want to talk about food or bulimia. She'd already shut down two other professionals with the silent treatment and was prepared to do it again.

I've been a student of human resistance, especially concerning adolescents, for many years. When a teenager comes into my office and I see the daggers she throws at me from her eyes, or notice him slump down into the sofa in my office, I know that person has no interest in being there and is only there because someone made them come. It is at this point that most of us adults who catch these nonverbal cues get defensive—in other words, we take it personally and make the resistance about us or we ignore it and move right ahead with our agenda. Both approaches will only increases the resistance.

The first task is recognizing the signs of adolescent resistance. We see it in

- apathy, or an "I don't care" attitude;
- tone of voice, for example, a hostile tone, using curt sentences;
- word choices and use of phrases such as, "I don't want to be here," "I'm being forced to be here," "Yeah, but…" as a response to something you've suggested;
- posture—resistance can be indicated by either an excessively withdrawn posture or an aggressive posture;
- facial expressions, such as smirks, eye-rolling, and raised eyebrows;
- refusing to accept a logical argument.

While all of these are signs of resistance, it would be wrong to interpret them as saying, "I'm never going to listen to you." A better way to see this is to read these signs as saying, "I'm not ready—yet—to communicate with you." The way we approach a teen who is exhibiting these signs will affect how we deal with the resistance.

Once when I arrived at a Catholic high school to speak at a general student assembly, I was greeted by a small group of students who asked, "Are you our speaker?" "Yes, I am," I responded. One young lady, who appeared to be a student leader, closed her eyes and begged me, "Please sir, for the love of all that is holy, can you *please* talk about something other than drinking and driving? We get the point. Every speaker for the last two years has talked about drinking and driving. If seven speakers didn't do the trick, I don't think number eight is some kind of magic bullet."

After I finished having a good belly laugh at her exasperation, I promised not to mention drinking or driving. These teens said to me, "If you talk about drinking and driving, we're not going to listen. So you're wasting your time and ours." They also communicated something else, without actually saying it: "We're willing to listen to you, and you have an opportunity to influence us by being the first person in almost two years not to harangue us about drinking and driving."

I shared my story with them and the message I had prepared. At the end of the assembly the principal told me he'd never seen his students sit in such rapt attention listening to a speaker since he began working at the school two decades before.

Many people hold an unspoken belief that when others don't respond to our verbal messages, be they suggestions, requests, or commands, if we say them louder or more frequently we will achieve the desired result. This belies a fundamental lack of understanding of people and the power of resistance. It also assumes that people make changes because of logic. Not so.

You may make minor changes in your life based upon logical reasoning, but most people cannot successfully make major life changes without an emotionally charged reason to do so. Often this reason is discovered within the context of a relationship marked by high levels of trust, caring, and understanding. Increasing the volume of our voice and the frequency of what we want to say only increases resistance and makes it that much harder to communicate our message.

If you've ever heard yourself saying, "How many times do I have to tell you?" or raising your voice with a teen (which is usually because we don't feel heard), that's a cue you're running into resistance. Depending upon the nature of your relationship with the teen, if you are a parent or teacher, you may be encountering this resistance while trying to handle an issue that merits a consequence. I will discuss consequences in greater detail in a later chapter.

There are four types of resistance that we may encounter with teenagers:

Intellectual. Having a different point of view, disagreeing with one's logic or reasoning, and ignorance. This type of resistance is falsely assumed by most Christian apologetics and thus explains why so much apologetics and evangelization is so woefully ineffective. It is the least prevalent form of resistance in young people today.

Spiritual. Sin is a choice to step out of relationship with Christ. The more seriously and repeatedly we do this, the more resistant we become to reentering that relationship.

Physical. Many people, especially males, experience, learn, and process kinesthetically—touching, moving, creating, and yes, even destroying. I've seen some highly resistant young people open up while mixing cement in Mexico, riding horses, or after they rocketed to the clouds as a result of jumping onto a giant air pillow in a mountain lake.

Emotional. This type of resistance usually results from an experience of disappointment coming from being wounded or let down. It is very common, especially with young people when they cannot place blame on someone or something else—as in the case of someone dying who was close to them, a natural disaster or tragedy, or a major disruption in family life such as divorce. When all else fails, the blame will either consciously or unconsciously be ascribed to God.

Saying, "I'm agnostic" or, "I'm an atheist" or, "Christians are just a bunch of hypocrites" are symptoms of emotional resistance that are often mistaken for intellectual resistance. These sound better than saying, "I'm having some feelings about God and the Church I don't understand," or, "I'm angry that God..." or, "My parents are divorced but I still love them both, and because I cannot give myself permission to be mad at them, I'll blame God for allowing them to get a divorce." Such awareness is rarely found in adolescents. Even those few who do possess such high levels of emotional awareness probably won't share it in a classroom, youth group meeting, or confirmation class.

You can make the most compelling case for apostolic succession, but if a young person says he hates the pope because he represents a God whom he believes took his father, you're wasting your time. The best way to address emotional resistance is to roll with it. Fighting it, arguing against it, or trying to persuade someone out of it will only increase its intensity and make your ministry (and possibly, your life) more difficult.

Young people who act resistant need acceptance and permission to be where they are and feel what they feel. Most importantly, they need to have a safe place to express themselves freely. If you become that safe place, you have the privilege of showing them a more accurate and loving picture of the God they resist. (All of the above applies not only to young people, but to young and older adults as well).

Do You Want to Be Right or Effective?

I once heard it said, "It's not good enough to be right. We must seek to be effective." You're reading this book because you want to be effective. Effectively influencing teens starts with meeting them where they are, not inviting them to us. Unless the situation is an emergency, give yourself permission to slow down, or postpone the discussion until you have the time and can muster the energy to empathize. If you don't you won't be influential and you will likely increase the resistance in the relationship.

When we get into repeating the same thing over and over, what young people (and any other age group, really) hear is, "It's all about me and my agenda. Listen carefully to me, because I'm right and I've got something important to say." That's not what we intend to communicate, but that's what young people hear. The fact is that too many adults will not lay down their agendas, as virtuous and noble as they may be, in order to have the opportunity to positively influence a young person.

Many adults get caught up in a need to be right instead of focusing on what they must do to reach teenagers. Being right is not the same thing as accuracy. Accuracy is an objective reality. Either the widget is or isn't green. If it is green, it is immaterial whether or not I acknowledge that it is green. The widget is green—nothing I say will change that reality.

Being right, on the other hand, is a subjective need of the ego. The green widget doesn't need you to advocate for its greenness, it will be green regardless. When you need me to agree with you or when you get upset that I don't agree with you, it's is a clear indicator that you are more concerned with being right than with being effective. Your need for someone else to see the widget, world, or even God the way you do comes from your ego's need to be right.

In relationships, the need to be right always interferes with experiencing intimacy. We narrow the criteria for connecting by saying "I can only be close to you if you agree with me." We can have meaningful relationships with others who don't agree with us, but it can only happen when we value the relationship more than being right. Very often, when you're dealing with issues in the lives of young people, you must value being effective over a need to prove that you are right.

There was a time when an unspoken rule existed to which most people adhered: that, out of respect, younger people would do what older people told them to do. There were other unspoken, societal norms concerning religious authorities: "Father says...," "Sister says...," "The teacher says...," carried only slightly less weight than Jesus's words in the Gospels. In short, there was a time when age and a position of authority were all that was needed to influence young people. Those days are long gone.

In response to such a reality, many cry, "But it shouldn't be that way!" Granted. But it is. We could fill up countless pages with things, situations, and changes taking place in the world that shouldn't be that way but are. And while we're bemoaning what shouldn't be, the reality of what is continues to worsen.

When you find yourself saying, "It shouldn't be that way," what you're doing, often unconsciously, is ascribing an unfathomable amount of complexity to a situation, issue, or problem that you believe must be a result of some cosmic force beyond your control. This gives you an excuse to not change, to not invest time energy and effort in understanding the nature of the problem, and to not act. In short, "it shouldn't be that way" is a cop-out.

When you find yourself thinking or saying that, use it as a cue to think, "I'm up against a problem I perceive to be so large and complex that I can't understand it and feel utterly helpless to influence." That is the reality, and naming what's going on inside of us when we encounter adolescent resistance (or any other seemingly insurmountable problem) is the first step to addressing it.

Once we acknowledge that, instead of saying, "It shouldn't be that way," we can say, "Right now I don't have enough information and skills to address this problem." Now you've opened a pathway to the solution. With more information, you will have increased understanding. And with new skills, you will grow in your confidence to address the issue.

Here are a few tips for recognizing and overcoming resistance:

Listen for the question behind the question. If someone asks about the abortion issue, before jumping into a defensive rant, ask, "Would you mind sharing with me (or with the group, if you are in that setting) your own feelings about abortion?" They're going to listen to you only after they feel heard and understood. What they really might be asking is, "Am I (or my friend, my mom) going to hell because I (or she) had an abortion?"

Practice the skills of active listening. Pay close attention to what is being said. Repeat back to the teen what you are hearing and ask if they feel you understand him.

Acknowledge and validate feelings and opinions. Everyone is entitled to their own feelings and opinions. Yet if you make one eye roll, one sneer, one disparaging sideways glance to another person in the room, you're toast. The teen will feel disrespected and this will only reinforce whatever feelings or opinions he or she currently has about adults, God, the Church, and Christianity.

POINTS TO REMEMBER

- Adolescents cannot act in a resistant way unless we give them something to resist.
- People, especially teens, want to be the expert on their own life. When you try to be the expert on their life, they will tune you out, whether you realize it or not.
- Instead of interpreting resistance as rejection, see it as a signal to listen better.
- There are four types of resistance: intellectual, emotional, physical and spiritual. Emotional resistance is the most prevalent form of resistance but is often mistaken for intellectual resistance.
- Focus on being effective instead of being right.
- Spending too much on getting teens to change gets in the way of changing the way you approach a teenager, which is the key to lowering resistance.

QUESTIONS FOR REFLECTION

1. Recall a time in your life when someone tried to convince you of something about yourself (or in general) you felt was not true. How did you respond to them? How did you feel inside?

2. Call to mind a teen either presently or in the past you've dreaded to see, work with, or talk to. What is it about that teen that brings up that dread in you?

3. When you encounter a resistant teen, what is your natural response? Become combative? Ignore them? Get defensive? Placate them? Detach from them?

4. Think of two people: one person who has deeply influenced you and one person who tried to influence you but who you tuned out. What made one effective and the other not so?

PRAYER

Lord, break down our defenses that we may reach out to others with patience, humility, and love. Help us to be gentle with the young people in our care, to see them as you see them—beautiful children of God. Amen.

CHAPTER FIVE

(*Hold Me in My Questions*)

+ When the Pharisees heard that he had silenced the Sadducees, they gathered together, and one of them, a lawyer, asked him a question to test him. "Teacher, which commandment in the law is the greatest?" He said to him, "You shall love the Lord your God with all your heart, and with all your soul, and with all your mind." This is the greatest and first commandment. And a second is like it: "You shall love your neighbor as yourself." On these two commandments hang all the law and the prophets." (Matthew 22:34–40)

+ C'mon man. Why are you standing there trying to answer something you know you don't know? I mean, do you think you're gonna be able to tell me how my parents' divorce or my grandparents death are a part of God's plan. If that's God's plan—I don't want anything to do with that God.

—High school sophomore

+ Owned faith does not mean that teens (or parents) will not have any more questions. Rather, questioning is the means to further growth in faith, coming to ever deeper understandings of God and the challenge of belonging to a community of believers.

—Robert J. McCarty[10]

Young people don't need us for answers. They can get better answers more quickly, efficiently, and better organized on the internet and from one another. What they do need us for is to help them form better questions. They need adults who can help them learn how to think and help them develop a Catholic imagination or perspective on life.

This chapter will discuss how we influence the world view of teens, how to handle a question that is really not a question, and practical tips for answering those difficult and loaded questions young people ask. Essential to this is not seeing oneself as a font of truth and answers, but rather as one who walks alongside young people, helping them to discover God's truth and God's presence in the midst of what is often a messy and tumultuous life.

If we believe that the desire for God is written upon a teen's heart, as the *Catechism of the Catholic Church* (27) says, then that will shape how we relate to teens. If we operate from a different assumption, we will feel compelled to fill them with answers and catechetical data—stuff they can find much more easily on the web. Teenagers don't need us for answers; they have the Internet for that. They need us to provide a context for the answers in terms of helping them to ask their deeper questions.

When I first started teaching religion to high school sophomores, I noticed that I had a deep feeling of frustration in me when I would go home after school. I knew I was working hard to present the material accurately and clearly. I welcomed questions from the students at almost any time during the class.

On one day in particular, it felt as if I were banging my head up against a wall. Jacob, a bright, sixteen-year-old young man who was the kind of class clown teachers liked, asked me, "So, Mr. P., are you saying that the difference between a divorce and an annulment is that in an annulment, my parents' marriage never existed?"

I proceeded to whip out my *Catechism* and read to him directly from the section referring to divorce and annulments.

Almost as if he didn't hear a word I said, Jacob asked, "So if my parents' marriage never took place, what happened at the wedding ceremony? What does that mean for my sister and me?" Missing the boat again, I launched into a carefully nuanced diatribe about how his parents were not "free" to give themselves to one another, which could have been an impediment for the sacrament to take place.

It was then Jacob looked at me with sad eyes and said, "I just can't respect a Church that says my parents' marriage never existed."

Years and many religion classes and students later, it dawned on me that my teens were not concerned about the Church's teaching. What they really wanted to know was, "How does a good God allow such a bad thing to happen to my family?" "If God is so good, Mr. P., and loves me as much as you say he does, then why did he allow my parents to divorce?" When I tried to answer these kinds of questions with a lecture on free will and why bad things happen to good people, my words would be ignored.

I soon learned a lesson that would serve me well even today in my work as a counselor: you cannot answer an emotional question with an intellectual answer.

Teens often ask "Why?" type questions. Wanting to maintain our credibility with them, we do our best to answer such questions. But underneath even those deeper questions lie more questions, such as "Why is life unfair?" "When will I stop hurting like this?" "Will my parents ever get back together?" "Will I end up divorced like them?" "Is it possible for me to be happy and then all of a sudden have my world fall from underneath me?"

Even here it is important that we don't quickly offer glib and cheap answers. Just because these questions are coming from teens does not mean that they are not mature questions about life, faith, and love. Teens know there is no easy answer to these questions. When we try to placate them with one of the cliché answers they've heard before, they'll write us off as insincere.

What they need in moments like these are adults who can recognize what's going on, get in the messy trenches with them, and help them make sense of the mystery of suffering.

Before trying to answer any question from a teen, try mirroring back to him what you heard him saying. (We talked a bit about this technique in a previous chapter.) Try to rephrase the question or summarize the essence of the question so it matches the content and the emotional intensity therein.

If a teen asks, "Why don't Catholics believe in abortion?" you might mirror this by saying, "Let me see if I got you. You want to know why the Church does not support a woman's right to abort her baby." Some teens will answer yes to this question. But I've also heard a wide variety of responses when I've used this technique. Some teens will say, "Yeah, but I guess, you know, it's her body, and she should be able to make that choice."

LACIE'S STORY
One day when I was still teaching high school, I was talking to the class about a pro-life position and abortion. Soon Lacie, one of the students, raised her hand. As I called on her, I noticed, but disregarded, the grimace on her face as she prepared to ask her question:, "So, let me get this straight, the Church teaches that abortion is wrong, right?" My response was, "Yes, it does. The taking of any human life is inherently wrong."

"Well, I just don't agree with that." she said.

"What would your life be like today if your mother had aborted you?" I said.

"Well I guess I wouldn't be here then, would I? And since I was a baby I guess I'd go to heaven. And besides, at that age you don't feel it anyway," she snapped.

As I began to respond I felt the irritation building up within me, and knew that my tone of voice was going to match hers: "So I guess if the person doesn't feel anything, that makes it OK to kill other people? So if I have in my desk twenty lethal doses of morphine, and injected them into your arms, you'd die but wouldn't feel a thing. That would be OK, then, according to you?" I quipped.

The majority of the students in the class nodded in agreement with me, a few just didn't care, and several others agreed with Lacie. At that point, with a sad, resigned look, she said, "Never mind."

"No, really. I challenge you to respond to that," I said.

"You win, Mr. P.," she said. After she said that I noticed several girls around her who looked at her compassionately. They didn't say anything, but looked back at me. I made a facial expression that said, "What's going on?" and they shrugged back as if they didn't know what was wrong. But their intuition had told them something was wrong.

Lacie just stared down at her desk. Moments later the bell rang and she, followed closely by a few of her girlfriends, practically sprinted out of the room.

Two of her friends came to see me during their lunch break that day and informed me that Lacie had just found out her older sister was pregnant. They thought it might be a good idea for me to talk to her because she seemed to be taking it really hard. This was a compliment to me, and I recognized it as such. After the discussion in class that morning, many teens would have written me off as just another adult, Church talking head who just didn't get it. I thanked them for coming to me and promised to follow up with Lacie.

Knowing teens as I do, I didn't want her to feel like I was making a big deal out of it, so I wrote Lacie a note and gave it to her last-period teacher, asking her if she wouldn't mind stopping by my classroom before she went home.

Lacie's facial expression on walking into my classroom indicated that she really didn't want to come. I got up, closed the door, and motioned for her to have a seat near my desk, and said to her, "I'm sorry. Period. I didn't know."

"That's OK," Lacie said. "I mean, how could you have known?"

"I don't know, but that's irrelevant. I'm sorry. You wanna talk about it? It seems like it's really bothering you."

"Well…I mean…it's no big deal, just drama, Mr. P. Everyone's got drama," she said, trying to downplay it. This is very common for teens who are afraid of becoming emotionally overwhelmed, and who are not sure yet if they trust the adult who is asking the questions.

"I hear ya," I said. "But I'd like to hear about the drama if you're willing to share it with me. It'll stay between you and me."

Lacie then told me that the previous evening, her older sister, who had just turned eighteen, confessed to her parents she was pregnant and was considering an abortion. Though Lacie was in her room, she heard every word, as her parents and sister were screaming back and forth. At some point the screams gave way to tears, and the last thing she heard her sister say, between sobs, was, "My life is over."

"That must have been tough for you, to hear all that," I said.

"Yeah, I love my sister so much, and I don't want her life to be over. And of course I hate it when any of us fight," she said.

"What is she going to do?" I asked.

"Not sure. I texted her and said that I loved her, but haven't heard back."

"Well, I'm here if you need me or if you just wanna talk about it. And again, I'm sorry for how I handled the situation in class today," I said.

"I understand. Thanks Mr. P., it's nice to know you care." Lacie gave me a half smile and left the room.

For the next several weeks I thought about Lacie and her family's situation. But what I mostly thought about and couldn't get out of my head was my behavior that day in the classroom when I tried to provoke a discussion about abortion with Lacie. I kept asking myself, "What did I miss?" I pride myself on "getting" my students and having a good rapport with them, but I had clearly missed something that morning.

At one point, I talked with a mentor about what had taken place; when I was finished he looked at me knowingly and smiled. He then asked me something I will never forget: "What was the question behind the question?" What did that mean, "the question behind the question"? I felt as if our conversation was becoming a scene in the movie *The Karate Kid*, with my mentor playing Mr. Miagi and I playing "Daniel san," and we were delving deep into the mysteries of life. "I don't know what you mean," I finally said.

"What was the real question she was asking you?" he asked again. "Uhhh, I'm stumped Obi Wan, help me out here," I said and grinned. "What made her ask you that question? Don't you think she knew the answer?" I thought for a moment, "Well. Now that you mention it, yes. I guess she did."

Lacie had been in a Catholic school all her life, and by now she knew what the Church taught regarding life issues. "So, in light of that, what do you think she really needed from you?" he asked. "Maybe to talk about her sister?" I said. "Maybe, but do you think she would have wanted to air that out in front of the whole class?" he asked.

Now I was beginning to see where he was going. "Sometimes," he said, "the question young people ask us and the question they're really asking are different. Related, but different." As we talked I began to understand that Lacie didn't care much about the Church's teaching—something that is true for the majority of teens today—she cared about her sister.

What Lacie was really asking was, "Is my sister a bad person because she's thinking about having an abortion?" and, "What will happen to her in God's eyes if she goes through with it? Will she burn in hell? Is my sister an evil murderer?" I spent twenty minutes of class time answering a question to which she already knew the answer. So what could I have done differently?

THE QUESTION BEHIND THE QUESTION

In matters of faith, teens will often ask questions that, on paper, seem like they have a simple catechetical answer. Even in the more murky waters of morality, there are a set of clear and concise answers that can be found in books such as the *Catechism of the Catholic Church* and *Youcat*. Teens know they can open these books to find the answers, and often they do.

Yet more often, I've found, they want to talk to us because they want to see if we have a different opinion from Church teaching, or if we can interpret the answer to their question in language they can understand. They ask us because inside most of them is a deeper question that is driving the one they're voicing to you, and they are trying to surface an answer to that deeper question.

What teens really want from us is to be held in their questions. How do we do this? First, it is important to understand the motive of the question. Teens' questions are less often a quest for answers and more often requests to connect, to be in relationship with us. All too often, adults miss that—as I did that day in the classroom—and in so doing miss an opportunity to connect with a teen.

So how do you recognize and elicit the question behind the question?

Refer to your basic understanding of teens: What are the issues going on in the lives of teens today? The research shows us that a significant majority of teens are facing issues of divorce, abuse, eating disorders, neglect, cutting, depression and other mood disorders. They are living in blended families, being raised by grandparents, exposed to the abuse of substances including drugs and alcohol, and developing over-sexualized behavior.

So if we know that the vast majority of teens are affected by or involved in these areas, we can safely assume that when they ask a question about any of these topics, there's a deeper question there. It's not guess work. It's a fact. In any random group of thirty high school students, regardless of demographics, there will be a majority of teens involved in or affected by one or more of the issues mentioned above.

Always ask "What do you think about that?" or "How do you feel about this issue?" Many adults are afraid to ask these questions for fear of what teens might say. This fear, while understandable, is unwarranted. You may be afraid that teens will criticize the Church or God, or you may worry that their opinion will influence other teens. Understand that for every teenager that asks a question or states an opinion, in my experience, at least ten other teens are thinking and wondering the same thing. Sometimes we may not want to hear the difficult questions and contrary opinions teens have because as long as they're not stating them, we can pretend they don't have these kind of questions. When we allow that question to come forth, we are faced with the reality that our teens don't necessarily share our convictions, values, and beliefs. Influencing this generation of teens demands that we elicit their questions and opinions regardless of how much they contrast with ours.

Check to make sure your teenager is understanding you. While this is a relatively simple thing to do, it takes an extra moment that we feel we may not have when the curriculum is breathing down our necks, or we have other children to attend to, or there are confessions to hear, or any number of any other urgent situations. Taking the time to make sure you're being understood is not efficient, but it is essential today. You can use this simple formula: "Let me see if I understand your question. You're asking..." or "I just want to make sure I know what you're asking. If I got it right, you want to know..." and then patiently waiting for the teen to answer that question.

Watch their nonverbal language. If they look away, or make a facial expression that says, "not really," while their lips are saying "yeah," they are really saying one of several things: "I don't want to be in the spotlight here, so let me just say whatever I think will get the teacher talking the fastest," or, "I don't have the energy to get into this right now," or, "No, that's not what I'm asking but I can't really ask the question I want to because I don't want people to know what I'm struggling with," or, "I don't want to make my mother angry by asking the question that's really inside me." These are all real concerns that we should be aware of.

It's important to allow teenagers to save face, but understand you'll need to revisit the issue soon without making it about them. One of the ways I've done this is to have a question box where students can anonymously drop in questions that they don't want to ask out loud in class or in person. This is a great tool for several reasons. First, it gives the teens a chance to ask these deeper questions. Second, you can find out what's important to them, what's on their minds and in their hearts. And finally, if I know what the deeper question might be I can pull a sheet of paper out of the box and pretend I'm reading that deeper question, then address it in my response.

Prepare for the question behind the question. There are ways we can prepare to answer the question behind the question when a teenager does not ask it of us or we deem it not the right time or place to solicit the deeper question from them or we sense that they wouldn't feel safe if we explored what might be the real issue. Many times the teens themselves aren't aware of what that deeper question is.

Here are some common topics with actual questions and the deeper concerns and fears.

- Is abortion a sin? What about abortion in the case of rape or if the pregnancy threatens the life of the mother?
- Is it a sin to have sex before marriage? What's really wrong with living together before getting married?
- Is oral sex a sin?
- Does the Church teach that you go to hell if you commit suicide?
- Why is it wrong to smoke marijuana?
- Why can the Church say that an annulment means a marriage never existed?
- Why does the Church hate homosexuals?

I realize that what I'm asking goes against the way many of us have been formed, that is, to get the answer right. Since our earliest days we've been rewarded for getting the answer right. Now, as adults who are responsible for teenagers, we may feel even more pressure to give them right answer to their tough questions. But remember that in every teen, underneath every question, are layers of other, deeper, and perhaps more significant questions. Answering the initial question too quickly may not allow enough space for teenagers to articulate their other, deeper questions.

Allowing time for the deeper questions to emerge will not feel efficient. At first it might seem like you're doing it wrong and wasting time. It is certainly easier to give intellectual answers to tough emotional questions than to allow the time to talk things through.

Yet giving an easy answer puts the relationship at risk—and the relationship is far more valuable than an answer. One answer gives me a moment of influence with a teen. A relationship opens up for me the possibility of a lifetime of influencing a teen. Which would you prefer?

POINTS TO REMEMBER
- When teens ask questions, especially about matters of faith, there is usually a deeper question burning inside of them.
- Helping young people grow in the faith and come back to the faith means that adults must be a safe place for them to express their questions, concerns, doubts, and fears.
- See questions as an opportunity for building a relationship instead of providing an answer, a chance to connect and invite teenagers to open up and go deeper.

QUESTIONS FOR REFLECTION
1. Looking back, has there been a time when I've been asked a question and responded but sensed I didn't really answer the real question? What might the deeper question have been?
2. In the teens I know, parent, or work with, what may be some of their deeper questions?
3. What is one thing I can do to make my home, classroom, ministry, or parish a safer place for teens to ask questions?

PRAYER
God our Father, keeper of all questions, help us be aware of the deeper questions burning inside the minds and hearts of today's teens. Give us the grace of compassion so that we can hold them and their questions in our care and, in so doing, lead them to you. Amen.

CHAPTER SIX (*Accept Me, I'm a Work in Progress*)

Jesus straightened up and said to her, "Woman, where are they? Has no one condemned you?" She said, "No one, sir." And Jesus said, "Neither do I condemn you. Go your way, and from now on do not sin again." (John 8:10–11)

I know my parents don't like my tattoos. But it feels like they just don't like me.

—High school freshman girl

We cannot change anything unless we accept it.[11]

—Carl G. Jung

It is a myth that good kids always make good decisions. Sometimes phenomenal young people make really poor choices. Think about your own life. You've certainly made some bad choices, as have we all. We can't expect that teenagers will have the same level of spiritual and moral maturity that we do. It took us many years to get to where we are right now, and with God's grace that growth continues. The same is true for teens: our task is to guide them through the process of spiritual and moral maturity.

One of the most common statements I hear from parents when they bring their child to counseling is, "But, Roy, we raised him better than that. He knows it's wrong to drink when he's under age, and he knows how we feel about that." Just because a teen made a poor choice doesn't invalidate his having been raised "better than that," and it doesn't mean they don't know right from wrong.

I sincerely give everyone the benefit of the doubt, and believe that everyone is trying as hard as they can to be his or her best self. Some people don't like this view. They think it's soft and allows too many slackers off the hook. But where does it get us to assume everyone's walking around giving a second-rate effort? It gets us nowhere.

Young people draw on a wide variety of sources, experiences, and knowledge to aid them in their decision making. Say a young person is considering whether or not to engage in premarital sex. In addition to the moral decision-making skills his parents have given him and the catechetical understanding of its immorality, there are other things he is considering as well. What will my friends think of me? What will my status be like if I do this (how cool will I be)? How much misery will this save me? What will this do to my body? What will I feel like when I'm doing it? What are the chances I'll get caught? What would happen to me if I did get caught? These are just a few of the considerations.

That young man knows it's wrong to engage in premarital sex.

Yet that knowledge alone is not enough to keep him from doing it. Even when accompanied by years of formation by parents who watched over him, modeled moral behavior for him, and showed him the importance of making good decisions, it's not enough. Nope. The fact that a teenager was raised "better than that" is often not enough to outweigh the power that acceptance by peers has in influencing a decision.

What does this tell us, then, about this teen? It tells us that he places an immense value on being accepted by his peers—which, to some extent, is normal for all teens. It tells us he's willing to risk the consequences of going against his parents' wishes and years of catechesis in order to be accepted by others.

Many adults will try to use the argument above, or an extended version of it, in an attempt to dissuade a teen from making a poor choice. This usually makes young people more resistant, however, because they feel they are not being listened to. If we were listening, we would hear how important it is to him to be accepted by his peers. We can then take that as a cue for continuing the dialogue about a healthy decision-making process, which is still being formed during adolescence. The soul is still growing, still assimilating new ideas and information, new experiences, along with the continual evolution of the adolescent self.

SPIRITUAL PRUNING

I love oak trees, and take special care of the two growing in my front yard. And as much as I love the look of a neatly pruned oak that has big, clean limbs, my arborist tells me that removing the scraggly branches just to make the tree look neat is bad for its health. Good pruning, he says, requires only that we prune away the dead wood, leaving everything else alone to live or die in God's time.

That makes sense. God designed the tree, and who am I to decide which parts are essential, which ones make the cut and which don't? But landscaping is not the only victim of my inclination to overprune. My desire for tidiness carries over into my spiritual life as well. There were (and are) times in my life when I wanted to root out parts of myself I didn't like, that didn't seem acceptable. It was only after some time that I came to see how these parts of myself were some of my greatest teachers.

I wish I could say I do this just to myself, but I don't. I sometimes bring my pruning business into the lives of the young people I work with, as well. Many times, busyness and my impatience with God's grace has caused me to prune away parts of who they are simply in order to clean them up and make them look good.

I'm not suggesting that we tolerate serious sin and problems in the life of young people or that we let our teens grow unattended while "God takes care of them." That is just another form of spiritual absolutism, another way of trying to keep life neat. And real life is never neat, especially when you are working with teenagers.

In my experience teenagers resist adults who cannot distinguish between a serious choice and one that's not as serious. We should be able to differentiate between choices like how long a teen wants his hair or the amount of makeup a teen wears and more complicated choices such as whether or not to have a sexual relationship before marriage, making poor choices in friends, using drugs or alcohol, causing harm to others, engaging in abusive practices, and other obviously unhealthy, sinful behaviors.

Our children are not ours, as heart wrenching as that may sound. Our most precious possessions are entrusted to us to care for, to watch out for. But ultimately, they belong to God, as do we. It takes great wisdom to recognize spiritual deadwood among the other healthy parts of their life. And it takes even more courage to refrain from overpruning.

Our call is to join with our children in order to help them discern the movement of God's Spirit in their lives. Instead of acting like bushmen whose job it is to hack our way through the jungle of their souls, perhaps we can see ourselves as responsible stewards who care for our Master's belongings.

Logical vs. Relational Consequences

Parents often ask me, "What's the one thing I can do to have a deeper relationship with my teenager?" If I were to recommend just one thing, it would be to understand the difference between logical and relational consequences.

A logical consequence means that certain actions deserve, or merit, certain consequences. When my five-year-old lies to me, that behavior merits a certain consequence. It may be a time-out or some other consequence that fits the behavior. Logical consequences are appropriate in intensity and duration with respect to the misbehavior.

A relational consequence is one that comes through in tone of voice, facial expression, or words. Instead of calmly saying, "Go to your room," we raise our voice and, with a look of disgust, say, "Go to your room! We cannot believe you let us down like this." There's a relational bite to the consequence.

Each of us is more than the sum of our behaviors: no age group is more keenly sensitive to this than teenagers, often in a negative way. If we're not careful when we react to an undesirable behavior, we can alienate a teen who confuses our criticism of their behavior with not accepting them as a person.

When teenagers do things that disappoint us, it can be incredibly difficult to accept, especially for parents. Most parents I know take their role so seriously and love their child so much that they tend to take personally their child's poor decisions even when those decisions have nothing to do with the parents. At such times it can be easy for parents to take out their emotional reaction, such as their disappointment, on their child. When this happens, what the teen hears is, "I am a disappointment to my parents," and not what was intended: "Your behavior disappoints and saddens me."

Too often, when we discipline our teens or administer consequences for some behavior, we unconsciously pass on a sense of shame to our young people, instead of helping them experience healthy guilt. Shame is sometimes thought of as a motivator, especially when it comes to moral behavior. But shame warps our identity; it does not come from God.

Guilt can be a good thing because it focuses on our behavior. When interpreted and administered correctly in a healthy conscience, guilt can move us into spiritual freedom. Shame, on the other hand, is about us and not about what we did; it's about who we are rather than a behavior, and that can be devastating. Shame paralyzes instead of freeing us, and binds us instead of opening us up into God's calling.

How do we effectively administer logical consequences for poor behavioral choices? We do so by using a positive tone of voice, speaking strong, solid words, and maintaining a loving facial expression. Much of what we communicate to others does not come through our words. Paralanguage, which refers to everything we use to communicate outside of words, is responsible for most of what is communicated to others.

This isn't to say that we shouldn't choose our words carefully. We should. But even more important than word choice are all the things surrounding the words we say. Facial expression, tone of voice, the way we move or don't move our hands, tilt our head, fold our arms, walk toward or away from a person when we're talking to them, our eye contact or lack thereof—these are all examples of paralanguage, and each of them affects the message we are sending to young people.

All too often, though, we administer relational consequences to young people. Our facial expression, our tone, and our words all say the same thing: "You've let me down." This hits a teen like a ton of bricks. And because it does, it is very effective at producing a behavior change. But let's think about the long-term fallout from that. I'm not suggesting that one misstep in discipline means a teen will need a lifetime in therapy. I am suggesting, however, that we can develop patterns in the way we administer—or fail to administer— consequences to young people.

Some might argue that most people, especially young people, don't notice things like tone of voice and facial expression while we're talking to them. In my experience, not only do teens pick up on these nonverbal cues, but they possess a hypersensitive radar that receives messages the sender may not even be aware she is sending.

I once watched a teacher whom I knew didn't really like teenagers try to discipline a classroom of high school students, telling them she really loved them and cared about them, and that she was doing this for their own good. You should have seen the eyes roll, the smirks, and the looks of disdain the teens had for this teacher! It wasn't because of the punishment per se but because they knew their teacher didn't like them. Being disingenuous about her love for them didn't help at all. On the other hand I've disciplined young people in the classroom, on retreat, and with clients, to great success because they know I genuinely love and care about them.

To review, here are a few things we should be aware of when disciplining teens:

Use non-inflammatory words. Teens are highly emotional, and a poor choice of words on our part can set up barriers to effective dialogue.

Have a positive tone of voice. Maintaining a direct and even tone to our voices helps to keep a situation from getting out of hand and allows us to get our message across without a lot of resistance.

Practice good facial expressions. Our body language and other nonverbal signs communicate the vast majority of what we want to say. We can use good words and have a positive tone to our voice—even though that is difficult to do if our facial expression is negative—but if our face is saying something else, it will negate the essence of our message.

Reinforce your message in good times and in bad. It is important for teens to hear what we think about them in times and situations that don't necessarily merit praise or chastisement. This will help build trust and go a long way toward alleviating any feelings that lead them to think, "They only love me when I'm doing something good."

The Need for Acceptance

It's very important for teenagers to be accepted for who they are—especially because they are a work in progress. Many of them are hypersensitive and can perceive, often with an accuracy that's scary, when they are being judged, which they feel is a lack of acceptance. Many teens today grow up feeling less secure and, subsequently, are more easily threatened by what they see as criticism of themselves. Because of this, it is critical that we do what we can to insure them that they are good simply by being who they are.

In Mark's account of Jesus's baptism, the voice emerges from the heavens and says to Jesus, "You are my Son, the Beloved; with you I am well pleased" (1:11). This scene occurs before Jesus has even started his public ministry or performed even one miracle! The Father proclaims his love for Jesus not for any miracle he has performed or parable he has told, but simply because Jesus is his

Son. The Father is saying, "It's not what you do that makes me love you, but who you are."

(I often wonder if Mary, prior to Jesus's public ministry, thought, "Geez! When's this kid gonna finally grow up and do something!?" I picture her shooing him out of the house, like a bird out of its nest.)

Isn't that what we all desire in life? To be loved for who we are, apart from what we do and don't do? Despite our successes and failures? To know that no matter what, we are loved at our core for who we are? This is especially critical for adolescents.

POINTS TO REMEMBER
- Our facial expressions, tone of voice, and word choice can determine whether we communicate unhealthy shame or healthy guilt to teens.
- Teens do not expect us to condone or approve of everything they do, but they do want us to accept who they are, despite what they do.
- If we're not careful in our attempts to root out bad habits and unhealthy behaviors in teens, we may unintentionally remove good elements of their personality.

QUESTIONS FOR REFLECTION
1. Recall a time when a trusted figure in your life used words or a tone of voice that was harmful as a means of trying to help you change a behavior. How did you feel then? How do you feel now? How might recalling this painful incident inform your work with young people?
2. Now think of a time when someone you trusted or respected demonstrated their concern about your actions or behavior in a loving and encouraging manner. Were you aware then of the effectiveness of their tone and approach? If not, what do you

now recognize about that encounter? How can reflecting on this encounter assist you as a minister to young people?

3. What are some of the conditions you use to reject others, whether consciously or unconsciously. How might these conditions influence your ministry with young people?

PRAYER

Lord Jesus, during your encounter with the woman caught in adultery, your tone of voice, word choice, facial expressions, and demeanor demonstrated your great love while offering admonishment and encouragement. Give me the graces of gentleness, compassion, and solidarity with the young people I hope to help grow into the fully realized sons and daughters of God you desire them to be. Amen.

CHAPTER SEVEN

(Console Me: I Do Care)

+ I was hungry and you gave me food, I was thirsty and you gave me something to drink, I was a stranger and you welcomed me, I was naked and you gave me clothing, I was sick and you took care of me, I was in prison and you visited me." And the king will answer them, "Truly I tell you, just as you did it to one of the least of these who are members of my family, you did it to me." (Matthew 25: 35–36, 40)

+ It is what it is.

—Any teenager alive

+ The inability during mid-adolescence to balance disappointment over specific events, people, or institutions by separating the good from the bad drives the intense need for a safe place. Mid-adolescents gather in like-minded groups to protect themselves from the forces they perceive as alien to them... [because] adolescents believe they have no alternative.[12]

—Chap Clark

Jason's parents sent him to me because his school had given him several detentions and was now threatening suspension because he refused to stand during the singing of the school's Alma Mater, which occurred weekly at the end of each school Mass.

The first thing I noticed about Jason was that he had a very distinct accent, indicative of people southeast of New Orleans, about a two-and-a-half-hour drive from Lafayette, which was where I lived.

"I can tell you're not from here, judging by your accent." I said.

"Yeah, I'm from Chalmette," he said while looking away.

"How long you been here?" I asked.

"Since the fall of 2005," Jason said.

To anyone living in Louisiana, that year was forever memorialized in our minds and hearts because it was the year Hurricane Katrina changed the lives of many in Southern Louisiana.

"So did you come here after Katrina?" I asked.

"Yeah," Jason said while still looking away.

"Tell me about it." I said.

"Ummm… Killer storm, smacked the hell out of us and changed life forever as we knew it," he said sarcastically.

"Touché," I said. "I'm sorry, I just wanted to know what that whole experience was like for you."

Jason began telling me how he had received a call from his mom telling him that the hurricane, which at one point had been headed further east, took a turn westward and was making a beeline toward the Mississippi and Louisiana coast.

Jason's mom, a lifelong resident of Chalmette, knew that a direct hit from a Category 3 or higher hurricane would mean they could lose everything. She told him to pack a bag and to make sure he put in it whatever valuables he wanted to save.

"What was in your bag, Jason?" I asked.

His eyes began watering. This tough boy, who would go on to

become a mixed martial arts fighter, was unsuccessfully fighting back tears.

"My grandfather's high school diploma," he said through a choked up voice.

"What school did your grandfather attend?" I asked.

"Holy Cross High School," he said. Holy Cross is an all-male middle and high school in New Orleans, founded in 1849 by the Congregation of the Holy Cross.

"What else was in the bag?" I asked.

"My dad's senior ring," he said, tears rolling down his cheeks.

"Where did your dad go to school?"

"Holy Cross."

"What else? In the bag—what else?" I managed to ask while fighting back tears of my own.

"My uncle's diploma."

"Let me guess. Your uncle also attended Holy Cross."

"Yeah, all the men in my mom's and my dad's family went to Holy Cross."

"So let me get this straight. You're about to be the first man in three generations who does not graduate from Holy Cross High School?"

With tears streaming down Jason's cheeks, his face changed from a look of sadness to anger when he said, "Yeah, and now these bastards want me to stand up and sing my love for their tradition. They don't know the first thing about tradition. I left tradition. My parents love it here, but I don't."

I sat with Jason as he pondered what he'd just said.

Jason looked across the room and stared at my crucifix and said, "Let me ask you a question. I see that cross on your wall. You must believe in God, right?"

"Yes, I do," I said.

"Look," Jason said. "Unlike all those kooks in the media who think God slung Katrina at New Orleans because of Bourbon Street, I don't believe that he caused it to punish us. But what I wanna know is this: Why didn't God stop it?"

I watched his expression turn again from anger back to sadness as he said, "He could have stopped it, right? I mean, he is God, right? I can't believe in a God who would so coldly turn his back on us when we need him the most."

"Yeah, he could have, Jason. And I don't know why he didn't."

I knew that this was an emotional question—a question of the heart, one for which an intellectual, catechetical answer would not suffice.

Pointing to the crucifix on my wall, I said, "And I also don't know why he didn't stop that either. But if you're open to it, I'd be honored to walk with you as we ask God to answer that question for both of us."

I would meet with Jason often over the next few years, and we explored that question and implored God's Spirit to answer it for us.

Not every teen has suffered the kind of trauma that Jason did. But most teens with whom I've worked can connect the dots just like Jason did. Whether it's a personal tragedy, a hurtful experience, or the pain of a friend or loved one, they all ask the same question: "Why wouldn't a good God stop such senseless suffering?" Without guidance, many of these teens slide into a passive resentment toward God and toward those who they see as representing God.

Disillusionment, Apathy, and Anger

I'm frequently asked, "How do we get kids to want to go to Church?" or, "How do we get kids to care?" Very often well-intended adults begin looking for a solution before they even understand the problem. In that sense it is better to ask first, "Why are teens apathetic? Why are they angry?" If we too quickly attempt to address the apathy or the anger, we'll get caught up in addressing the symptoms and not the underlying causes.

Underneath it all, and sometimes buried deep, teen apathy and anger is a broken heart repeating this mantra: "Someone, something, or some experience has hurt me, let me down, or disappointed me, and now I'm disillusioned."

Some will argue that disillusionment is a normal part of life, and wonder why it's such a big deal for teens today. That's a good point. The difference for teens today is that they are experiencing that disillusionment and unmet expectations at an earlier age than previous generations.

Today, young people are disillusioned on several levels:

Disenchantment with society. During the last twenty years there has been no shortage of disappointment and let down from public figures. Politicians, presidents, artists, celebrities, priests, corporate titans, and athletes have all demonstrated that human weakness is not isolated to those who are out of the public eye. People and institutions, the Church chief among them, who once unquestionably held the public trust today struggle to earn it back. Add to this mix a naturally skeptical teenager and you have a recipe for disenchantment.

Disenchantment with parents. Divorce, busyness, and the overall disintegration of the family that has occurred over the last two decades has taken its toll on young people. There is research to suggest that teens overall today are more resilient[13] and as such are adjusting to divorce better than before, yet it still takes its toll. Many teens I've worked with struggle to conceive of their life as resembling the traditional family.

Disenchantment with peers. This may surprise some people, but one of the greatest sources of disenchantment for teenagers is with their peers. Developmentally, teens need one another. They need one another like they need oxygen. They bounce off and rub against one another in the process of individuation, becoming an individual apart from their family of origin (parents, guardians, etc.). During this process there is deep longing for acceptance. For many teens, this need is met in different ways, but far too many walk the hallways of school and ride the bus home feeling alone, unaccepted, and ultimately excluded from the lives of their peers—which, for all practical purposes, is their life. This leaves them with a lingering sense of disappointment with others. In the language of one teen, "If no one cares about me, why should I care about them?"

Disenchantment with themselves. This is perhaps the most common and most insidious disenchantment, and it occurs when teenagers realize they are not who they once thought they were. For many teens, this feeling is rooted in deeper places of shame. As Becky puts it, "Before I was raped, I believed I was a good person. Now I can't see that person anymore. I just see someone who should have stopped him from doing that. If I were a good person, I would have stopped it." Then there's Alicia, always the perfect student who worked hard for every A she earned. When her standardized test scores came back lower than she thought, she began to doubt herself for the first time in her life. Her hard work had made a way for her, earned her respect from her teachers, attention from her parents, and the esteem of some of her peers. Now she would be faced with telling her classmates that she could not attend the school of her dreams because her scores weren't high enough to get in.

Disenchantment with God. Poor God; once the scapegoat, always the scapegoat. When all else fails, when there's no one else to blame, when we won't let ourselves blame anyone or anything else, God will suffice. This is especially true in the lives of young people. Teens will rarely say out loud, "Why did God allow Hurricane Katrina to happen?" or, "Why does God allow terrorism and war?" There's something in them that knows God isn't that ruthless. But like everyone else, they will ask the question: "Well, if God didn't cause it, then why didn't he stop it?" This is a tougher question to answer because it goes to the heart of the mystery of suffering.

GRIEVING UNMET EXPECTATIONS

There is a way for adults who work with teens to help them address the various disappointments of their lives and offer them a both a process and a spirituality for understanding and dealing with disappointment. This is the process of grieving.

Understandably, many think of grief as something one does only when they lose another person through physical death. But there are many other forms of grief that occur for a myriad of reasons, and often far less obvious reasons than the loss of a person. These steps can help teenagers address their grief.

Name the wound. This step helps answer the question, "Who or what was lost?" It deals with further questions such as "What was hurt inside of you?" "What's not going to happen now as a result of this experience?" "What difference has this loss made in your life?" "How has it affected you?"

Voice the expectation. When I was a child, I expected that, like most of the people I went to school with, I would have a mom and a dad. I expected at least that I would know who my father was. But I didn't. Other common expectations that teenagers voice are: "I expected that we'd be together until we both decided to break up."

"I expected my parents to be faithful to each other and love one another and never get divorced."

"I expected my friends to always be there for me."

By giving a voice to the expectation, teens grow in an awareness and understanding of why they are reacting the way they are and feeling the way they're feeling.

Express the feelings. There are common feelings associated with grief. These do not always occur in a specific sequence or in a linear fashion. Sadness, anger, frustration, disappointment, confusion, and abandonment are all feelings we experience when we lose something. One important role for adults here is to encourage teens and give them permission to feel and express their feelings. Some effective ways of expressing feelings are through crying, talking, writing, painting, or drawing.

Understand what forgiveness is. It is commonly thought that forgiveness is an event. It is not. Forgiveness is a process—a process that often looks like two steps forward and one and a half steps back. It usually happens in fits and starts. It involves choosing to go through a process of letting go of some *thing* that we feel we are entitled to hold on to—a thing that others would not argue our right to hold on to.

What's most important to understand about forgiveness is that it's a choice. I often hear people, teens included, say, "I don't feel like forgiving," to which I respond: "That's OK, because it's not necessary to feel forgiveness in order to begin the process." What's important is that the person be ready to make a choice and begin working toward forgiveness. Again, this is not something that teens need to understand in order to do; they don't necessarily need to know that they are discerning whether to forgive or not. What is important is that you, as an adult who is helping them in this process, must understand what's happening.

We cannot prevent bad things from happening to good people. As adults it can be especially disenchanting for us when we look underneath the masks of apathy and anger, and see a disappointed teen's heart. This can be especially difficult for parents, who see it as their job to protect their children from hurt.

Teens know and understand that we cannot protect them from all things that might hurt them. What they want and need from us is a willingness to walk with them through the uncertainty and messiness of grief, toward healing.

POINTS TO REMEMBER

- Teenagers today may seem apathetic to the adults who love and minister to them, but that apathy is actually disenchantment in disguise.
- Teens are disenchanted with various aspects of their lives and the society in which they live, perhaps more so than any previous generation. They are disenchanted with God, society, their parents, their peers, and perhaps most importantly, themselves.
- This last level of disenchantment, with themselves, is the most dangerous, as it can and often does drive a young person to seek affirmation, love, and security in places and from people that do not truly have their best interests at heart.
- Teens long to have the following needs met by those in their support systems: attention, feeling heard, intimacy, access to the sacred, and a safe place. When teens don't receive these at all or in a way that makes them feel safe, they will search anywhere and everywhere to fulfill these needs.

QUESTIONS FOR REFLECTION

1. Think back to your time as a teenager. Toward what or with whom were you disenchanted or apathetic? Did that affect your interaction with your family, your peers, your local community? In what ways?
2. How were the needs mentioned in this chapter met or not met in your own experience as a teenager? Where or with whom did

you seek to fulfill those needs that were not met by your support network?

3. What might be some effective and safe ways to determine the needs of the teens with whom you work? List one way you can practically meet (or begin to meet) the needs of the young people with whom you work.

PRAYER

Lord, make me an instrument of your peace. Where there is hatred, let me sow love; where there is injury, pardon; where there is doubt, faith; where there is despair, hope; where there is darkness, light; where there is sadness, joy.

O, Divine Master, grant that I may not so much seek to be consoled as to console, to be understood as to understand, to be loved as to love. For it is in giving that we receive, it is in pardoning that we are pardoned, and it is in dying that we are born again to eternal life.

CHAPTER EIGHT (*Disciple Me and I Will Follow*)

+ I give you a new commandment, that you love one another. Just as I have loved you, you also should love one another. By this everyone will know that you are my disciples, if you have love for one another. (John 13:34–35)

+ It's hard to believe in a God you can't see. It's like, I wanna follow Christ, but I can't see him. But I can see you. And I trust you. So...I guess if I hang around here and get involved I'll get to know Christ better. I dunno. I mean, its workin' for me right now. We'll see."

—*High school junior girl*

+ Maybe the best way to evangelize Millennials is by personally introducing them to a God who is bigger than their successes and failures within an authentic church community that offers refuge for their weary bodies, minds, and souls.[14]

—*Frank Mercadante*

If you were to ask a teen to follow you today, their first response would be "On Facebook? Instagram? Twitter? Where?" For young people today, the word *follow* has several meanings. For example, they follow one another on Instagram, Twitter, and other media sharing sites. But in that sense the word follow means "keep tabs on," "track," or "keep up with." It's not quite the same as our more common understanding of "to go, proceed, or come after," or "to engage in as a calling or way of life," or, as we'll talk about in this chapter, "to accept as authority."[15]

What does it mean to disciple someone, especially a young person, today? Most of us are familiar with the scriptural accounts of Jesus's early disciples, who left everything to follow him: "Jesus said to them, 'Follow me and I will make you fish for people.' And immediately they left their nets and followed him" (Mark 1:17–18). But in a world where young people are constantly connected to each other and overly available, how can we invite them to follow us in order to lead them to Christ?

The truth may seem obvious: You cannot lead others to places you have not first traveled yourself. Yet if you've spent any amount of time trying to invite others to journey with Christ, you know how easy it is to forget this simple truth. If we are not attempting to live and model what we are inviting teenagers to do, we have no hope of them following us—especially today's generation of teens, who value authenticity and transparency so highly.

Disciples are women and men of prayer. They understand that reaching out to teens begins not when they encounter a young person to whom they are ministering, but when they encounter the Lord in prayer. This is such an important facet of discipleship that Jesus modeled it often for his disciples: "Now during those days he went out to the mountain to pray; and he spent the night in prayer to God" (Luke 6:12).

Prayer helps us to:

Clarify our roles. Raising teens or working with teens is a complex process that often involves multiple roles, including that of mentor or friend. As teens grow in maturity you are able to have more mature conversations with them and perhaps get more satisfaction from the relationship. Yet as quickly as you can snap your fingers, they revert back to being a teenager and you have to put on your adult hat again. The flexibility between these roles can be very difficult to negotiate. Prayer helps you to clarify what your teen needs most from you at this time in your life.

Steady our emotional responses. As I've mentioned before, the biggest reason the teenage years are so difficult is that their minds, hearts, and bodies are growing rapidly. Prayer helps us to find a grounded center from which we can reach out to them. As one teen told me, "I know I'm all on the Rockin' Roller Coaster! I don't need her (Mom) to come along for the ride!" Although they don't show it, teens often know when they're emotionally turbulent, and they need the adults in their lives to be steady, centered, and collected. Prayer will help you do this.

Model the importance of prayer. Teens are always watching us. I was interviewing a high school junior boy for a position on our campus ministry retreat team, and asked: "Why do you want to do this ministry?" His response was unrehearsed: "Well, I watch my dad pray real hard. I don't get what's happening when God and him are talking, Mr. P, but they're talkin' bout heavy, deep stuff. I wanna talk to God like that."

Caveat Emptor: Discipleship Is Messy

While riding a bus home after spending a week doing mission work in Mexico with a group of teenagers, I watched a tear roll slowly down Dawn's sunburned cheek. The double Whopper value meal I was inhaling at the moment was the first taste of Americana I'd had in seven days, but it was going to have to wait. I'd seen that look before.

In a choked-up voice Dawn, a chaperone on this trip along with me, said, "I feel like I just wasted my Easter break. I thought these kids were 'getting it' but they didn't get anything. They're the same—they may even be worse than they were when we brought them to Mexico a week ago!"

"Why do you feel it was a waste?" I asked.

"Haven't you heard the kids talking? Arguing over snacks, gossiping, back in their little cliques? Nothing's changed!" said Dawn.

I nodded empathically and said, "I hear ya, Dawn. Look, I know they look the same, but they're not. Water before it's boiled looks exactly like it does after it's boiled, but it's different. It's been changed. These are not the same teens we brought to Mexico," I assured her. For the next couple of hours on the bus ride home, and while finishing my double whopper, we talked about why we may not see an immediate change in behavior when our young people are exposed to a profound spiritual conversion experience.

Discipleship is messy. It was messy among Jesus and the first disciples. Among the twelve, there was treachery, deceit, jealousy, ambition, sloth, fear, greed, and pride, to name a few struggles of the early, hand-picked followers of Christ. Yet many adults are appalled when teenagers coming home from a mission trip or sharing supper after a weekend retreat stand around gossiping and arguing over who gets the largest slice of pizza.

Teenagers need to come up for air after intense experiences like camps, retreats, and mission trips. As adults we have a better capacity to stay in the moment and process these events, understanding what they might mean for us and how that should impact our lives. But most teens will return to normal teen behavior immediately after such events because their soul cannot hold the intensity of such experience for as long as adults can.

Instead of seeing their normal behavior as a sign that they weren't changed by the experience, we can choose to see it as resurfacing from the event, a chance to refill their lungs with air so they can go deep again. Our discipleship challenge after such events is to be intentional about following up with them, inviting them to revisit that deep place again.

It takes time to integrate the Gospel into one's life. The more resistant a teen is, the slower this process will be. We set ourselves up for real disappointment when we expect teens' spiritual and moral development to happen in a steady linear fashion. It's not to say no one develops this way, but in my experience working with today's teens, most of them do not. True discipleship, true holiness is the work of a lifetime. It's positively dangerous to use a checklist mentality in assessing spiritual and moral development. That box you check today might be unchecked next month or next week even.

Monitor and Adjust Expectations

When you grow frustrated with a teen's seeming inability to "get it right" or "get it together," that can be a good time to move inside yourself and ask, "Why is this teen or this situation bothering me so much?" Your initial answer to this question is likely to be, "Because I love this teenager too much to allow them to continue living like this." That's a good answer. But I invite you to stay with it longer and see if there are other, perhaps deeper, reasons why you want someone's behavior to change.

A few years ago, I was the spiritual director for Janet, a youth minister. During the course of our work together, she was facing the challenge of working with a particularly resistant sophomore girl whom Janet had accompanied to a summer camp run by the girl's school. At the camp, Janet and the girl had built a relationship, and the teen had given Janet permission to follow up with her during the school year.

As with many teens who have amazing spiritual experiences over the summer, this young woman met her first real challenge in October at a party after the school's homecoming dance. Janet heard a rumor that the girl had smoked marijuana and was sexually promiscuous that night. Not wanting to rely on hearsay, Janet visited the girl, and during their conversation, she confirmed the rumor Janet had heard. This was a blow to Janet, and she found it difficult to contain her unhappiness with the news. The teen sensed Janet's disappointment with her and began withdrawing.

At our next spiritual direction meeting, Janet brought up the conversation with the teen. I asked what had bothered her the most about the teen she was working with. Janet replied, "Well, I invested all that effort in her, and she blew it at homecoming! She had no respect for herself that night!"

"When you say she 'blew it,' what do you mean?"

"You know what I mean, Roy," she said, frustrated.

"No, no, I don't, actually. Blew what? What did she 'blow'?" I asked.

"I don't know. It's just that she went and did that after having such a good summer."

As Janet and I continued to visit, it became clear she was unaware of her expectation that after all her hard work, her teen disciple should have been perfect. And when the girl failed to meet that expectation after the homecoming dance, Janet was distraught and began to question the meaning and effectiveness of her involvement with teens.

I helped Janet to see that her reaction was an essential revelation for her both as a Christian and as a minister. Over the next couple of years, during our spiritual direction sessions, we discussed how Janet might adjust her expectations of others—and herself—to be more realistic and healthy.

We avoided both extremes: demanding perfectionism on one hand and allowing unrestricted license to do whatever one wants on the other. This enabled Janet to act as a safe place for teens who were struggling to do the right thing, but who occasionally succumbed to temptation, while at the same time being a voice of challenge to those who were not trying to live a Christian life. This allowed her to maintain a sense of integrity as a minister and as a disciple of Christ who wanted to disciple others.

We all have expectations of the young people in our lives. The problem is that most of us are not aware of our expectations; they are unconscious. What do you expect from the young people you disciple? When you ask them to follow Christ, to follow you, what are you expecting from them? These are hard questions to answer because they force us to quantify moral and spiritual growth.

When we answer these questions about what we expect, we might hear ourselves responding that we want our teens to sin less and do more good deeds. If we pay attention to what we are thinking, we might actually realize how silly that sounds in contrast to how Jesus enrolled the first disciples. He didn't have a tally sheet for sin and good deeds for his new recruits. And while he did say "for each tree is known by its own fruit" (Luke 6:44), there is no evidence he had conversations with the apostles about their behavior.

There is also a danger in leading teens to believe that we will or can meet their expectations of us. I'm not talking about what type of pizza will be served or what time to meet for coffee, but the deepest of expectations: "Will Roy ever disappoint me the way my dad disappointed me? Will he do anything to make me feel let down or abandoned the way my mom did?"

Our ego wants to rush in to soothe their anxiety (and ours) by assuring them that we will always be there for them and not let them down. But this reaction is dangerous and unhealthy, because you cannot promise that you will always be there for a teen, especially if you do not know what that means for them. Furthermore, you cannot promise that you won't let them down because you have little, if any, control over that. Whether a teen is disappointed or let down is largely their own choosing, not yours.

Finally, even if you were able to perfectly meet their expectations, it remains important for teens to know and learn, especially while being mentored by caring responsible adults, that disappointment in others is foundational to life. It will happen regardless of how hard you try to avoid it.

Follow My Lead

An important piece to remember with Christian discipleship is that Christ invited his disciples to follow him. He did not invite them to follow the Church, or a set of rules, laws, or codes, as good as all these things can be. Jesus knew that people follow people; that same principle holds true today. This is especially true for teens. As I've mentioned before, they are a disillusioned and disenchanted generation. They want to follow someone, but they don't want to follow someone who is going to let them down.

Part of the disenchantment teens often feel with others comes from their unconscious reflective disappointment with themselves. At this point in their lives, they are beginning to become capable of letting themselves down, and they are becoming aware of the fact that they can let themselves down. This is a deeply saddening awareness for anyone but especially for a developing teenager whose ego needs to feel bulletproof and perfect.

One day David, a teen who sometimes participated in campus ministry at the high school where I worked, stopped by my office. I could tell he was nervous and that something was off. When I asked if he was OK, he said, "Yeah, I'm fine." But I could tell that he wasn't fine. Teens say that to test the waters, expecting us to know whether they're fine or not and to see if we really want to know.

So I said, "Are you sure? Because you don't seem fine. I know what fine looks like on you, and this isn't it." I smiled knowingly, looked him right in the eyes, and paused, giving him tacit permission and nonverbally asking him to tell me what was going on, or at least attempt to tell me what was happening.

David said, "Ugh! It's so stupid," which usually means it's awkward or embarrassing. "It's nothing, I'm making a big deal out of nothing." This sort of comment always follows the initial comment that something feels embarrassing, and it's a teen's attempt to retract what they've said already, and head back in the other direction to save face and ease the awkward feeling. As adults, if we're not aware of what's going on and if we're not comfortable with the awkward feeling ourselves, we'll allow them to do just that, or even worse, help them do it ourselves and miss a crucial opportunity for connection and growth.

I said, "OK, take a deep breath. It's OK. First of all, remember my rule: nothing, *nothing* is stupid—except trying to make a veggie burger look and taste like a piece of meat; that's stupid—but other than that, nothing is stupid. It can be a little embarrassing and awkward at first to have HDRC's (heavy, deep, and real conversations) but it doesn't have to be if you know it's a safe place. Right, David?" I asked, wanting him to look me in the eye, which he did. "This is always a safe place."

I didn't think David had anything serious on his mind that day, but I handle all interactions with teens this way because each small interaction is a test for those that are potentially more serious. The lighter interactions are toe dippers, testing the water to see if it's safe. And if a teen feels that indeed it is, they'll return to talk about more consequential matters later.

David said, "Well, I just dunno. I'm confused."

"OK, I hear that," I said, nodding empathically. "What exactly are you confused about? Or is that the problem?" I half smiled.

He chuckled, "Well, yeah that's part of the problem! I just don't know what I'm supposed to be doing here. I get the feeling I should help out in campus ministry, but I'm not really even a member of campus ministry. I feel like you..."

Here David stopped talking and gave a deep sigh. I knew where David was going here, and gave him permission to say what he needed to say and what I needed to hear. "Say it, David, say what's on your mind. You have nothing to be afraid of—I want you to say exactly what you're thinking. It's going to be OK."

"I feel like you want me around, but I don't know if you do or not. Sometimes I get that impression from people and I'm wrong and I make a fool out of myself. And I'd rather just go away. I don't want to be in the way if I'm not wanted."

You have to know what amazing courage it took for this young man to be that vulnerable to utter those words. I'd wanted to say these same words to mentors several times, but could never find the strength to say them.

He saw the tears well up in my eyes at what he said. I was hammered by his vulnerability, and he yanked me, almost unwillingly, into a similar place. My tears had answered his question, so, not wanting this seventeen-year-old, testosterone-filled male to feel overexposed emotionally, I purposefully brought us both up for air by saying, "Nope, this is all a sham. I don't even work here, actually. I'm an undercover agent for the CIA trying to infiltrate the Vatican from the ground floor up, from the bottom. I figured this was the best place to start."

I stood up, and we walked out of my office, side by side, which allowed him to feel less exposed. While we were walking I said, "I do want you here. If you want to be here, I'd like you to join me." David said yes.

The lesson I learned from David is the same lesson Cardinal Newman tried to teach us years ago with his motto, *Cor ad cor loquitor*, "Heart speaks to heart." When we risk being vulnerable, we risk being hurt. But we also open ourselves up to love, surprise, intimacy, and adventure. When we close off, when we are not vulnerable, we'll still get hurt—it's part of being human. But we'll also miss out on love, intimacy, and adventure.

David risked putting his heart out there by asking, "Do you love me? Do you want me? Do I have something to offer?" and found a resounding "yes" at the end of his question.

Many teens will not be so vulnerable, and even with the ones who are, it may be difficult for you to understand what they really want from you. In times like these it is helpful to know that all teens want acceptance, inclusion, affirmation, and validation. You can assume that the teens you have access to are around you because on some level, perhaps a level they do not themselves recognize, they want to be around you: they want to follow you. If they did not, they would be someplace else. It is our responsibility to take the initiative of inviting them and reinviting them into a journey of discipleship. While they are on that journey with us, we can validate them and affirm them in their decision to follow Christ through our guidance, ministry, and teaching.

POINTS TO REMEMBER
- In order for us to invite teens to be disciples of Christ, we must take our own journey as disciples of Christ seriously
- Just as Jesus invited the early disciples to follow him, we too invite teens to follow Jesus through us.

- Holiness is the work of a lifetime. Teens cannot hold the serious tone of spiritual experiences as long as most adults can and will often act out or go back to their usual behavior immediately following such experiences. This does not mean the experience wasn't real or effective.
- Teens want us and need us to personally invite them to journey with us as disciples of Christ.

QUESTIONS FOR REFLECTION

1. Reflect on your own journey of discipleship. How did you come to faith? Who was instrumental in inviting you? Challenging you to follow Christ?
2. Which people were less effective in reaching you? Why?
3. In what ways might you authentically do the same with the young people in your life?

PRAYER

Lord Jesus, you made true disciples of your followers by your example of compassion, integrity, and selfless giving. Help me to make disciples of the young people I work with, not with words but through human action touched by grace. Let me be a living witness to the authentic discipleship that can only come from a life of personal and communal prayer. Amen.

CHAPTER NINE

(*Permit Me to Struggle with Faith*)

+ When the man saw that he did not prevail against Jacob, he struck him on the hip socket; and Jacob's hip was put out of joint as he wrestled with him. Then he said, "Let me go, for the day is breaking." But Jacob said, "I will not let you go, unless you bless me." So he said to him, "What is your name?" And he said, "Jacob." Then the man said, "You shall no longer be called Jacob, but Israel, for you have striven with God and with humans, and have prevailed." (Genesis 32:25–28)

+ I know this may sound weird—and, like my parents, you might not believe me. But I really am a spiritual person. I have morals and religious beliefs. And no, I don't like going to church and would not go if my parents didn't make me. But that doesn't mean I don't believe in God, and it doesn't mean that I don't respect Catholicism. And it doesn't mean I'm not searching for answers I don't really have the words for.

—High school junior boy

+ To have the courage to let ourselves be embraced when we are sinful and bitter is to first of all know a God who...is both a blessing Father and a caressing Mother, who sees with the eyes of the heart, and who, despite our weaknesses and angers, sits completely relaxed, smiling, with a face like a marvelous symphony.[16]

—Ronald Rolheiser, O.M.I.

It can be difficult, if not nearly impossible, to walk with someone who is struggling with matters of faith if we ourselves have never struggled with our faith—or perhaps more accurately, given ourselves permission to struggle with our faith.

Too often we associate the word *struggle* with weakness, or at worst, sin. Some of us feel that if we are struggling with a matter of faith, then we must be weak. We might even think we don't really love God, because somehow we have the idea that people who love God do not struggle with God or faith. These thoughts and feelings usually happen outside of our awareness, but in my experience many people, especially those who minister in the Church, are plagued by them.

It can be difficult to acknowledge these thoughts and feelings because when we articulate them we expose the perfectionism that lays beneath them. What on the surface might appear to be a noble attempt to work out one's relationship with God is usually masking an egocentric need to be perfect.

The spiritual path of young people will certainly take them on a rollercoaster ride of doubt, confusion, anger toward God, self-doubt, apathy, and skepticism, along with passionate belief, integrity, and commitment. When working with teens, it's important that we recall the difficulties of our own spiritual journey and see what parts of their rollercoaster ride resonate with our own journey. If we are not willing to do this we risk becoming too demanding, too rigid and inflexible, and we might be seen as having unhealthy expectations for adolescent faith development. Remember, it's always two steps forward and one step back!

Sometimes we think that if we ignore the fact that a teen might be struggling with his or her faith, then they will simply stay in an unquestioning relationship with God—as if we have any control over that, anyway. What really happens when we do this is we reinforce the fact that we are uncomfortable with their struggle, rather than inviting them into a place where they can share their questions and doubts. We are denying them—and ourselves—the opportunities to share our own struggles with faith, and how our beliefs were reinforced through the struggle.

We cannot make young people feel love for God any more than we can make a duck bark. By virtue of the Christ who dwells in them, they already love God. The God in them loves the God of them. Remember that, because it's true for you, too.

We can easily fall into the mode of Christian warriors on a mission to fix others, to change their unbelief and negotiate their struggles for them. But Christ never asked this of us. I know this is hard to see, especially for those of us whose personalities are such that we live to help others. We see it as our gift. But it's almost like trying to see the air around us: we cannot.

Christ calls us to a ministry of presence with teenagers. Can we be present to them, be with them during this time of struggle? Can we attend to the rollercoaster ride that they are on? This can feel to us like powerlessness; many people will read right over this paragraph and move on to do some real ministry—planning, fixing, doing, straightening out, defending, changing—instead of letting God guide our efforts. Our actions sometimes say, Who needs God when our teens have us?

FEELING POWERLESS

It can be difficult and sometimes painful to watch teens struggle with a faith and God you have come to love, especially if they are your own children. One mother said to me, while describing her son's struggle, "Roy, how can a boy who loved the Lord so much as a child turn his back on God now, at a time in his life when he needs God the most? It feels like he's throwing away everything we've taught him."

While I caution parents against identifying with or living through their children, I also think it's impossible—and in fact, unhealthy—not to do this to some degree. I know of no parent who truly loves his or her child who doesn't at some point overly identify with that child, and make the child's problems their own problems. You actually have to hold on to something—in this case, a teenager's struggles—before you can let them go.

Here's how it works. In the beginning of life, young people are totally dependent upon their parents and others to meet their needs. They grow gradually, often fitfully, into independence. And while a great deal of attention is given to the difficulty adolescents have is becoming independent, not much is said about the toll this takes on the adults who love them, raise them, mentor them, and minister to them. What then is required?

Faith development in the teens we raise or care for continually asks us to let go. This can feel like dying, or like being powerless; it may seem like an uncomfortable vulnerability or uncertainty. During these years many parents are plagued with newfound or intensified self-doubt, asking themselves (and anyone else who will listen) questions such as "Am I doing the right thing?" "Am I letting go too soon?" "Should I jump in now or wait?"

Too often, the emergence of these questions and doubts can make us feel we're doing something wrong. Yet it is precisely the opposite. If we can enter into the struggle with our teens, it can bring about a similar transformation in us and a deepening of our own faith—although this might look very different from what our teens are going through.

The rub comes in identifying when it is appropriate and necessary to let go, and how much to let go of. There is no handbook that outlines the appropriate age or level of letting go that may be necessary to help a teen resolve their faith struggles. There is no magic age where we no longer identify with, live through, and make personal our children's struggles.

But just because we feel powerless does not mean we really are. We may experience the reality of having less of an ability to control our teenagers as a feeling of powerlessness. The truth is that seldom are we really powerless. We may be powerless to have others do exactly what we want and to have situations or people turn out exactly the way we want them to. This is the reality of life. But in the vast majority of situations and relationships, we do have the power or ability to influence our teens.

The best way for us to influence teens during times of struggle is to dialogue with them. By definition, teens are absolutist and especially today, transparent. Their motto might be, "I must take a bold, rigid stance toward life and proclaim this to the world." When we enter into a dialogue that is motivated more by our curiosity than by a desire to persuade, we can help them contextualize their bold, rigid stance within the language of struggle.

FAITH IS A SAFE PLACE

Sometimes a teenager's struggle is really a cover for their need to discover and actualize who they are apart from their parents and other adults. For some teens their own faith is the only place they feel any freedom to exercise their autonomy. As one teen told me, "Technically, while my parents may not like that I'm agnostic, it's not something they can punish me for. They may still nag me about it and make me go to Church, but they cannot make me believe in something I don't want to believe in." For this teen, faith, religion, and spirituality are safe places for him to assert his autonomy.

It's both normal and necessary for adolescents to seek freedom and autonomy. What teen doesn't think they can handle more freedom than they actually can? And while they are often not ready for the amount of freedom they deem appropriate, they have a legitimate need to experiment with pushing boundaries and asserting their autonomy. It might be helpful to think of it like a beach ball submerged in the water that you are holding down with your hand. As long as there is air in that ball, it will seek to rise to the surface. We can hold it down, but eventually it will rise to the surface.

When Alissa's parents brought her to me, they listed several of the concerns they had about her, anxiety, depression, and self-harm among them. But the last and most important to them was that she was questioning her faith. This deeply troubled Alissa's parents, and they begged me to do something, anything, to "straighten her out" on this subject, if I could.

In our third session together, after Alissa began warming up to me, I asked, "So, Mom and Dad asked me to chat you up about God and all things holy," ending with a chuckle.

She replied, rolling her eyes, "O. My. God. I know."

"I figured this was not a subject you were inclined to discuss," I noted with a smile.

"OK, no, not really. At least not in the way we 'discuss' it at home," Alissa said.

The dialogue continued: "How do you guys 'discuss' (using my fingers to make air quotes) at home?"

"Well, the 'discussion' (she was now making quote marks with her fingers) involves them telling me how much I should love God, how I should never question a priest because they're perfect, and because priests can't have sex, we should be nice to them and do whatever they say. They also tell me I should love going to Mass, which I find boring as hell. And if I want to start World War III, or am having a masochistic bout, I participate in the 'discussion' and offer an opinion or ask a clarifying question. But usually I just nod and say, 'Uh huh,' and, unbeknownst to them, pray that they shut up. That's our discussion."

"Sounds fun!"

"Break out the chips and dip… It's a real party."

"Sounds pretty over the top. I can only imagine. Do you think they know how you feel about God? Church? Them?"

"They know I'm not happy. They think I'm going through a phase, and maybe I am." This is an uncharacteristically mature statement from a sixteen-year-old, that is, the ability to consider herself as the problem. It's not something most teens can do.

Alissa continued, "But I don't think it's a phase. You see, Mr. Roy, the thing is, I don't have a problem with God—under no circumstances are you allowed to tell them that. I have a problem with my parents' God. It's like they're brainwashed or something. It's hard to take them seriously when they say things like, 'Don't question a priest' or, 'we must pray for gay people because they're handicapped.' I don't think they've ever met a gay person. They'd probably go wash their hands afterward if they ever did, afraid to catch the 'gay disease.'"

Here I smiled in an attempt to convey acceptance to Alissa. I don't need to agree with her or disagree with her: I just need to accept her because this is where she is at the moment in her feelings about herself, her parents, and God. As you'll see, this is not a bad place for her to be right now.

Alissa asked me, "What do you think?"

I said, "I think you know what you think and feel, and why. I think you are who you are, and you are where you are. What do you think?"

"I think at times my parents and other adults get in the way of God instead of leading us to God. Jesus said, let the children come to me. Well, we would if they would just move out of the way."

At this point in our session, I wanted to turn on a video camera because I was well aware that Alissa was exceptional in her understanding of herself at that age. It's not so much that her experience is exceptional, but her ability to articulate it at this age is truly exceptional and seldom experienced by adults, especially parents. Like most teens, Alissa doesn't comprehend the enormity of responsibility that comes with either parenting or ministering to young people. So it only makes sense that her reaction comes by way of oversimplifying a very difficult and complex process, namely, getting out of the way, a process we touched on earlier in this chapter.

Alissa's story also compels us to look at how we can get in the way. As I have said in several other places, our getting in the way is usually unconscious, outside or underneath our awareness of the situation. I don't know any caring adults who consciously try to interfere with a teen's developing relationship with the Lord. In fact, it often comes as a humiliating shock to realize that our attempts to lead our teens to Christ are backfiring and possibly doing the opposite of what we had intended.

In Alissa's case, her parents were shoving Jesus and the Church down her throat, and she was choking on it. Fortunately, I was able to work with the family and help her parents to see that their best efforts to keep Alissa engaged in the Church were having an opposite effect on her. In their minds, if they just held on to their tactics long enough Alissa would see the light and internalize the faith in the same way her parents had.

I helped her parents to see how their own faith had developed over time. Ironically, both of them had left the Church for a long period of time as young adults, up until Alissa was four years old. At that point, they attended a marriage retreat and had an experience that opened their eyes.

As I helped them articulate their experience of that retreat some twelve years earlier, they were able to see how their time away from the Church was accepted not only by the staff but by God. During an intense spiritual experience at the retreat, they were able to leave what they described as a bad place for them, both individually and as a couple, and to return to a more active embrace of the faith.

I asked them to think about how that experience would have been different if they had felt unaccepted and judged by the staff. They immediately said, "It wouldn't have worked. We probably would have bolted." After recounting this experience, Alissa's parents were able to make a connection between their own experience and their daughter's struggles with faith, without much help from me. They were able to see how God always, always meets us where we are. Only after experiencing that unconditional acceptance does the truth of God's love beckon us to grow, to a conversion of heart.

"I guess we haven't been too accepting with Alissa," her Dad said with a slight chuckle, as he soaked in his realization. "I guess we were just so afraid she would leave the Church like we did, abandon God like we did, that we just wanted to do everything we could to prevent it. And now it looks like we created exactly what we wanted to avoid." I told Alissa's parents that it took no small amount of humility to acknowledge that.

I met with Alissa's parents a few more times to help them map out a way they could practice acceptance of their daughter while being true to themselves and their roles as parents. We discerned that attending Mass each weekend as a family was a reasonable expectation for anyone living at home. I helped her parents find ways to dialogue with Alissa, using curiosity and acceptance as guiding principles in lieu of persuasion and intolerance.

No situation is ever perfect, or works out perfectly, even the ones that seem like it from the outside. This one was no different.

Alissa had to work on ways to forgive her parents and allow them to do their job as parents. Her parents had to continue finding ways to recognize and acknowledge their own fears without reacting to Alissa's changing spiritual and emotional needs. And while they are still navigating these waters today, Alissa has become a peer minister at her high school, something she chose to do so without her parents' encouragement. Because her parents were able to relax their need for her to own the faith, she was able to embrace it with autonomy and integrity.

It can be difficult, especially for parents, to watch those they love most in the world reject the faith that means so much to them. Yet it is important to remember that our desire for having our children remain faithful can slip into us forcing it to happen. When we slip into forcing it, we forget that God's grace is the initiator of faith, and we risk causing further distaste for matters of faith and religion in our teens' lives.

Practicing watchful, hands-on acceptance of a teenager's struggle with God and the Church allows them the freedom necessary to take ownership of their faith.

Points to Remember

- Struggle is a normal and necessary part of faith development, without which one cannot deeply and personally own their faith.
- It is not our job to remove struggle from teens, but to journey with them, encourage them, dialogue with them, and give them hope during these times.
- It is helpful for adults to remember their own struggles with faith in working with teenagers, thus creating a more accepting and nonjudgmental relationship.
- Faith can be a safe place for teens to test the waters as they begin to assert their autonomy.

QUESTIONS FOR REFLECTION

1. Reflect back on your own faith development, and remember a time when you struggled with God or faith. Was there a person who was helpful to you during that time? What was it about them or how they related to you during that time that was especially helpful?

2. What are some practical ways you can offer a solution of acceptable compromise to your teenagers, whether as a parent, teacher, or minister? In other words, how can you meet them in the middle when it comes to their faith journey, not forcing them to adhere to your own paradigm of spirituality while also gently guiding them in their spiritual development?

PRAYER

Lord, like Jacob and the angel, we sometimes wrestle with the young people in our care, holding on to our own expectations of who they should be and how they should act. Give us the grace of faith to continue the struggle and the wisdom to know when and how to yield to the experiences of our teens. Bless us and them with the graces you want us to receive, not those we expect or believe we should receive. Amen.

CHAPTER TEN (*Teach Me: I Want to Learn*)

+ Then Jesus said to the crowds and to his disciples, "The scribes and the Pharisees sit on Moses' seat; therefore, do whatever they teach you and follow it; but do not do as they do, for they do not practice what they teach.... You have one teacher, and you are all students. (Matthew 23:1–3, 8)

+ I learned a lot, I guess in her class. But I learned most of all how much she cared about us. You could tell we mattered to her—more than just our grades.

—A high school sophomore girl talking about her religion teacher

+ Handing on faith must mean sharing our love for [Christ], and not just information about him. We forget that catechesis is this straightforward. We fall prey to the myth that teaching is a display of competence rather than an act of love.[17]

—Kendra Creasy Dean, Almost Christian

Not everyone who reads this book will identify with the role of teacher or catechist. Yet we are all charged with teaching the faith. Jesus commanded us to "go into all the world and proclaim the good news to the whole creation" (Mark 16:15). Having been entrusted with the faith ourselves, we are responsible for passing that same faith on to younger generations in whatever our particular role or setting.

If you're reading this book, it is because in some way, God has placed you in the life of a young person or young people, be it as a parent, godparent, catechist, youth leader, catechist, minister, teacher, mentor, or other. And while you may not have a formal setting from which to teach, be assured that you do indeed teach the faith, every day.

A saying that's been attributed to St. Francis of Assisi is, "Preach the Gospel at all times, and if necessary, use words." Teens are always watching us. In fact, they are watching us more closely than they are listening to our words. They watch how we treat them and how we treat others. As such, most of what we teach teens about Jesus happens not with words but in how we conduct ourselves, how we approach teens, how we treat them and react to them and their friends.

There are countless studies showing that the overwhelming majority of communication happens through paralanguage—that is, everything we do other than our word choice. Our tone of voice, facial expression, posture, pacing, and demeanor are all speaking loudly before, during, and after we utter any word. Because of this we need to pay attention to how we are modeling Jesus in our lives, for that teaching speaks louder than any formal lesson.

One of the advantages of not being a formal teacher is that teens aren't automatically resisting you. With formal teachers, they know what's coming, so they prepare themselves; they know what to expect and are ready to resist.

In my role today, as a counselor, young people don't see me as a formal teacher. This gives me a huge advantage when it comes to sharing matters of faith with teens and connecting faith to the struggles they are experiencing in their lives. Informal teachers are effective for the same reasons that teens write off their parents and listen to the advice of other adults, who tell them the exact same thing their parents tell them: teens don't see it coming. They're not expecting it. They don't see you as having an agenda and aren't prepared to resist you. Therefore you can be effective—sometimes, more effective than a formal teacher.

Nurturing the Desire for God

As we noted in an earlier chapter, the *Catechism of the Catholic Church* says that the "desire for God is written in the human heart" (CCC 27). This means that ours is not the task of giving God to young people but of pointing to the God who already dwells within them, who is already at home, and whose spirit is at work within them.

If the *Catechism* is correct, then it must be true that, deep down, young people do want to learn about God. I've mentioned this several times in previous chapters, but it bears repeating here since it is the basic premise of this book. Despite verbal and nonverbal communication to the contrary, teens really do want us to teach them about the person of Christ. Our real task in working with teens is to clear away the clutter and cobwebs and help them identify and articulate what they most deeply want: to better know God through Christ.

What does it mean to teach a young person about the person of Jesus Christ? The word *educate* comes from the Latin word *educare*, which means "to lead out." Regarding the teenagers in our care, then, we are tasked with leading them out of the darkness of their lives and into the light of the Gospel of Christ.

When we teach Christ, students will learn. And while that seems obvious, if you've taught the faith for any amount of time at all, you're no doubt familiar with the countless distractions that keep us from performing this simple task consistently. It's very difficult to keep things simple and perform them consistently, and it requires a great deal of effort.

To teach Christ assumes that we ourselves know Christ. It assumes that we have a close relationship with Christ formed through personal and communal prayer, the study of God's word, and the great tradition of the faith.

When we're in a position to share faith, to share Christ with teens, we must also be currently working on our relationship with Christ. Having a relationship with Christ is no different from any other relationship—the foundation of which is care for the other, nurtured through communication—talking, asking, and listening. If we are not actively working on our own relationship with Jesus, teens will sense this and be less inclined to hear what we have to say.

Christ is compelling, and likewise, your own experience of Christ is compelling. You don't need to dress it up, add bells and whistles to it, or exaggerate it to make it attractive. When we genuinely and authentically share our knowledge and experience of Christ, teens will listen. They won't be able to help themselves. They will walk away from our teaching and say, "Wow. Jesus is real."

One of the reasons teens are attracted to the person of Christ and want to learn more about him is because in some way, almost always without realizing it and being able to name it as such, they see their story in the Christ story. This universal fact was noted by the Second Vatican Council: "Christ, the new Adam, in the very revelation of the mystery of the Father and of his love, fully reveals man to himself and brings to light his most high calling" (*Gaudium et Spes*, 22).

BE ON GUARD AGAINST DISTRACTION

Meetings, grades, curriculum, discipline problems, issues with clergy, students, parents, and administrators: all of these are traps for teachers. All of these activities can lure us in and take our time away from what should be our primary focus: teaching Christ to young people. Steven Covey said it best, "The main thing, is to keep the main thing, the main thing."[18]

I used to keep a sticky note on my desk that reminded me of what my job was: "Teacher = Be Christ for Students." And seeing Christ in our children and students helps awaken all of us to the Christ in our midst. It's that simple really. There are countless methods, pedagogies, and techniques for doing that, but the hardest part is remembering, day in and day out, that what we are called to do when we accept the call to teach young people is to help them see Christ in their midst. This is more important than the fact of any curriculum, dogma, rules, commandments, or dictum: we are teaching the person of Jesus Christ.

When we invest time in teaching and knowing the person of Christ, the young people who may have been just snoring will wake up! They will hear it in our voices as we read the Scriptures, they will feel it in their hearts as our awakened faith knocks loudly on the door of their dormant soul. They'll find themselves sitting up, awakened by the same Christ in us who is also deep within them— even when they don't know it or believe it.

Young people don't want to be a number, or just another face in the crowd, no more than does any one of us. We all want to be an individual to other individuals. We want to be truly seen by others as unique and special. This is true no matter how we are teaching our teens—in the home, in a classroom, in youth ministry, whatever the setting.

At the start of my first year teaching religion in a Catholic school, I was assigned five classes, each with between twenty-seven and thirty students. I wasn't prepared for the daunting task of teaching and ministering to 140 unique individuals every day, in fifty-minute intervals. And while today I have opportunities to speak to audiences of thousands and people often comment how good I am at remembering names, I wasn't always that way. As with most things, I learned the hard way.

There was a young woman in my second-hour class whose first name I had a hard time pronouncing. I tried to get it right a couple of times, but after the second week, I gave up. I rationalized this by saying, "I'm just embarrassing her and myself by my repeated attempts to pronounce her name correctly, so I'm just giving up." For the rest of the semester, I called her by her last name, "Ms. _____." She was the only student out of the thirty in that class whom I called by last name.

Over the course of the semester her grades were average, but I'd heard from other teachers that she was an exceptionally bright and hard-working student. After she made a D in my class for the second grading period I called her parents and asked if they'd meet with me to discuss her religion grade.

Her parents were very kind at our meeting and listened attentively to my concern. The mom said, "Mr. Petitfils, I would imagine that growing up, you had to have been picked on about your name."

"Yes," I said immediately. "I still am, actually," laughing a bit.

"I would imagine," she said with a smile. "So I'm sure you can understand how important pronouncing someone's name correctly is to them. In the grand scheme of things, we know this is not a big deal, and we have talked with our daughter about this several times, but she is hurt that she is seemingly your only student whose name you won't bother to learn. Of course she can do better than a D. I'm just surprised she didn't do worse."

I felt my heart sink into my stomach at that moment because I realized that because I hadn't taken the extra time to learn how to pronounce my student's name and practice pronouncing it, she was shutting down on me.

The next day, I asked her to meet me after school. She came in to my classroom, head hung low. "I heard you met with my parents," she said. She sighed from embarrassment, which I acknowledged.

"I just want you to know I feel really bad about not learning how to pronounce your name," I told her. She could tell by the look in my eyes and my face I was genuinely sorry. "I had no idea. I know you're a freshman, a new student this year, and there are a lot of things you're learning, huh?"

"Yeah," she said.

"Well, I'm a freshman teacher. And there are lot of things I'm learning too. I just wish I could have learned this one without hurting your feelings. You don't deserve that." She half-smiled at that. "So," I said, in a slightly upbeat tone, "Can we start over?"

"Sure."

"Can we switch roles for a few minutes before your ride comes? You're the teacher and I'm the student. Teach me your name."

As you might imagine, after that her grades soared for the remaining two grading periods.

Names are important; they are the tools that help us identify things. Shakespeare's point about "A rose by any other name would smell as sweet"[19] is valid for many things, because changing the name of something does not change the thing. This is not true, however, for people and relationships. Your name is part of who you are; it speaks to your identity.

In the Book of Isaiah, God says, "I have called you by name, you are mine" (43:1). Jesus reiterates this in the New Testament when he says, "I am the good shepherd. I know my own and my own know me" (John 10:14), and, "He calls his own sheep by name" (John 10:3). It is comforting to know that God cares for each of us so much as to know us and call us by name. If we are to share that same God with young people, we should work hard to do the same and call them by name.

CONNECTING FAITH TO THE PERSON OF CHRIST

One day after class, a student named Tyler said to me, "See, the thing is, Mr. P., when you explain it like that, I want to know about Jesus. I wanna learn about him. I jus' don' wanna know 'bout all 'em rules 'n stuff. I jus' don't see God in all that."

What Tyler was saying, in his unique way, is not uncommon among young people. They hunger to know more about the person of Christ—the personality of Christ. What was this man like? What is this God like who would take on human form? Too often, for many different reasons, their impression of faith is learning doctrine and "thou shall nots" instead of learning about the person of Christ and the face of God. And while we adults may be able to make the connection between the person of Christ and the teachings of the faith, that connection is lost on many young people.

A former student once approached me in a store and said, "Mr. P., I don't know if you remember me, but I was in your freshman religion class. I just wanted you to know that you probably thought I was a bad kid and didn't like you. But I was listening to every word you said."

I started to interrupt him, but he said, "Wait, let me finish. You know, I wasn't the least bit interested in what you were teaching. I wasn't even Catholic. My parents made me go to that school because it had good academics. I thought I was going to have to suffer through four years of people beating me over the head with the Bible—well, you guys are Catholic, so whatever it is, you beat us Protestants over the head with, hahaha. Anyway, I didn't even want to hear about Jesus. My parents shoved Jesus down my throat enough, and I thought, great, here's one more person to do it."

"But you didn't do that. I could tell right away something was different in your class. It took me a while to figure out what it was, but I was thinking about it the other day and wondered, 'What was it that Mr. P. did that made me want to listen? What did he do that made me want to learn?' I realized it was two things: You cared about us, first, and you cared about what you were teaching, second. Both are important, and the sequence is important. I cared about what you were teaching because I knew you cared about me."

"And," he continued, "that changed my life."

One of the dangers of teaching faith is that we run the risk of allowing our passion for the subject to override our passion and love for the people with whom we are called to share it. What this student was telling me was that I (on this occasion) did not allow this to happen. He was clear that I cared primarily about my students. Because I cared about them, I wanted to share with them something I loved very much: my faith.

This is subtly different from caring so much about my faith that I want to share it with everybody. It's not that the latter doesn't work sometimes, because it does. But in most settings where we will teach teens, the dynamics of the size of the group and the frequency we meet with them highlights our priorities. If we are to be effective with teens, we must understand that they know instantly when they are or are not the priority.

When our ministry is to teach them and minister to them, we must maintain focus on our love of them. Our care and concern for them must be our priority. When that's held in its proper place, sharing the faith will happen naturally and effectively.

Be Christ to young people by seeing Christ in young people.

I once watched a video of Mother Teresa speaking to a group of new postulants. Elderly and frail at the time, she was wheeled into the room and looking up at the bright, eager young faces she said, "You all aspire to be Missionaries of Charity; this is what we do. We wake up in the morning and we go before Jesus and adore Jesus in the Eucharist. And then we go to Holy Mass and receive Jesus in the Eucharist. And then, we go out into the streets of Calcutta and we seek Jesus in his most distressing disguise, in the poorest of the poor. That is it. If you want that, stay. If not, go. I don't need you."

That is what good teachers do, too! We go out and seek Jesus, who is often disguised as an apathetic, questioning, skeptical, resistant teenager. Toward the end of my years in the classroom, I would pray at the beginning of each day: "Lord, help me to see you, disguised as each one of my students, their parents, and my coworkers today. But especially in my students." As teachers, whatever our setting, whatever our role, we pray for the eyes of faith, to see as God sees, with the eyes of the heart so that we might see through to the heart of each one of those young people God places in our care.

God is a person in Jesus Christ. Jesus lived an adventurous, countercultural, and dangerously threatening life. He left behind stories, principles, and examples of how we can have the same. I am convinced that sharing this Jesus with our teens, this radical, nonconforming Jesus, is totally compelling to a generation of bored and busy teenagers disillusioned with adult generations and institutions, especially the Church.

As we invest time in prayer and study to know this radical Jesus and attend to his gentle movements in our own life, the economy of our teaching will change. The once numerous brood of bored, apathetic, and argumentative teens will turn to reveal captivated, awakened, and docile believers longing to know of whom you speak.

Gradually, those same teens who once ignored and fought you will draw near to you, docile to the Spirit reaching through you, to the same Spirit who dwells within them.

POINTS TO REMEMBER

- As Catholics who follow Jesus, we are all called to hand on the faith to others.
- We cannot talk authentically and passionately about someone we do not know. Make it a point to know Jesus and teach that person to the teenagers in your life.
- Teach people—don't teach a student or a class, but teach individuals with their unique learning styles and wounds and needs and issues. If you teach in a classroom, do your best to learn the names of your students and their story. They will return the favor by learning from you.

QUESTIONS FOR REFLECTION

1. Who are the teachers, whether by profession or function, who have taught you about Jesus? How did they reach you most effectively? How can you incorporate those methods and approaches into your own ministry?
2. What are some authentic and practical ways you can preach the Gospel without using words, as St. Francis advised, in your ministry?
3. Are there any young people you minister to whose names you have not yet learned or whose stories you don't yet know? If so, what can you do to remedy this in a practical and safe way for you and the young person?

PRAYER

Jesus, divine teacher, give me the grace to witness to you by the way that I treat myself and others, especially those you have placed in my care. Grant that my interaction with others and the way I live my life may be proof that I am your companion so that like St. Paul, I can be "all things to all people" to people to whom I minister (1 Corinthians 9:22). Amen.

Conclusion

Raising teenagers is like trying to nail Jell-O to a tree.

—Unknown

If there was only one idea you could take away from this book, it would be this: Despite the emotional, intellectual, physical, and spiritual turbulence that surrounds them, more than anything else, teens want meaningful relationships with healthy adults. When they cannot get that, they will settle for other people, things, and experiences.

Teens want adult input in their lives and guidance through the obstacles life presents them. Even though this happens amid the backdrop of an exploding insecurity, which can appear as defensiveness and resistance, it is essential that during this time parents, ministers, and other adults remain engaged with the teen.

Teens need our attention. This is a basic human need that we often take for granted when life gets busy and other things become urgent. Young people need to be truly seen by meaningful adults in their lives. Seeing them, especially the parts of them they are afraid to show us, validates them. Contrary to what some suggest, as humans, our greatest fear is not rejection per se, but being ignored. When we attend to young people by initiating relationships with them, by smiling at them, by treating them like they are important, we affirm their presence as worthwhile.

Teens have a voice they long to be heard. We all need to feel heard, but this is especially important for children and adolescents. Hearing a young person involves more than simply listening to them. It involves a commitment on our part to listen to them until they feel heard—and very often until they become clear on what they are trying to say.

And while teaching the faith is important, we must remember that we are always teaching young people about who God is by sharing with them who we are. Teens do not need us to acquire religious data—they have the Internet for that. We must ask, "What can we offer teens that they cannot Google?" We give teens, through the appropriate sharing of our experience of God and community a context, a life story within which they can better understand the truths of our faith.

Teens need us to be a holding ground for their pain—a safe place that respects their growing need for autonomy, appropriate risk, and adventure. They need us to initiate frequent invitations to walk with them down the winding and often confusing paths of this life, constantly reminding them of the hope we share of our fulfillment of life eternal. They need to experience in us, the incarnational love of Christ that "bears all things."

This is not to say that teens need us to be God for them. It does mean that they need us to be a bridge leading into a God we know personally. They need us to answer their difficult and often controversial questions with more powerful questions of our own that challenge them to grow deeper in awareness of themselves, others and God. They need us to facilitate dialogue that brings them into and holds them within a tension that respects the messy, often unclear grey areas of life that. They need us to offer them more than simplistic, self-help clichés and trite, tired, and often defensive apologetics and to represent to them a tradition that is alive.

Teens need us to work harder on acquiring and developing skills to dialogue with them in ways that honor their resistance, addresses their skepticism, and persists through their defense mechanisms. They want to know, understand, and really believe in the faith we share. But this generation demands that we be proficient in our ability to effective impart the faith. We must be real about who and what we are and be really good at being open to who and what they are.

Finally, on behalf of the many teens I have worked with over the last twenty years, thank you. Thank you for taking the time and making the effort to read these pages and for even considering how you can improve on the good work you do with teens. May God continue to bless our efforts as we minister among his young people.

Notes

1. T.S. Eliot, "The Dry Salvages," *Four Quartets* (Orlando, Fla.: Harcourt, 1943).
2. Chap Clark, *Hurt: Inside the World of Today's Teenagers* (Grand Rapids: Baker, 2004), p. 143.
3. Clark, *Hurt*, p. 187.
4. Clark, *Hurt*, p. 190.
5. Frank Mercadante, *Engaging a New Generation: A Vision for Reaching Catholic Teens* (Huntington, Ind.: Our Sunday Visitor, 2012), Kindle ed.
6. Ron Rolheiser, O.M.I., *Against an Infinite Horizon: The Finger of God in Our Everyday Lives* (New York: Crossroad, 2001), p. 38.
7. "Suicide Prevention," Injury Center: Violence Prevention, Centers for Disease Control and Prevention, http://www.cdc.gov/violenceprevention/pub/youth_suicide.html.
8. Sue Monk Kidd, *The Secret Life of Bees* (New York: Penguin, 2003), p. 185.
9. Kidd, p. 92.
10. Robert J. McCarty, *Raising Happy, Healthy, and Holy Teenagers: A Primer for Parents* (Washington, D.C.: National Federation for Catholic Youth Ministry, 2001), p. 76.
11. C.G. Jung, *Modern Man in Search of a Soul* (Orlando, Fla.: Harcourt, 2011), p. 234.
12. Chap Clark, *Hurt 2.0: Inside the World of Today's Teenagers* (Grand Rapids: Baker, 2011), p. 61.

13. For example, Michael Ungar, *Playing at Being Bad: The Hidden Resilience of Troubled Teens* (Toronto: McClelland & Stewart, 2007).

14. Mercadante, p. 56.

15. Merriam-Webster Collegiate Dictionary, 10th ed., s.v. "follow."

16. Ronald Rolheiser, *The Holy Longing: The Search for a Christian Spirituality* (New York: Doubleday, 1999), p. 241.

17. Kenda Creasy Dean, *Almost Christian: What the Faith of Our Teenagers Is Telling the American Church* (New York: Oxford University Press, Kindle ed., 2010).

18. Kevin Kruse, "Stephen Covey: 10 Quotes That Can Change Your Life," *Forbes*, July 16, 2012, http://www.forbes.com/sites/kevinkruse/2012/07/16/the-7-habits/.

19. Shakespeare, *Romeo and Juliet*, Act II, Scene II.

About the Author

Roy Petitfils is a counselor at Pax Renewal Center for individual, marriage, and family therapy, and taught at the high school level for more than ten years. He is a popular speaker and workshop facilitator, and works with the National Federation for Catholic Youth Ministry. He is the author of three books including *What I Wish Someone Had Told Me About the First Five Years of Marriage*.